Open
In Case of
Emergency

Open
In Case of
Emergency

Mike Rampton

POP PRESS

3 5 7 9 10 8 6 4 2

Published in 2020 by Pop Press an imprint of Ebury Publishing,
20 Vauxhall Bridge Road,
London SW1V 2SA

Pop Press is part of the Penguin Random House group of companies
whose addresses can be found at global.penguinrandomhouse.com

Copyright © Mike Rampton

Mike Rampton has asserted his right to be identified as the author of this
Work in accordance with the Copyright, Designs and Patents Act 1988

First published by Pop Press in 2020

www.penguin.co.uk

A CIP catalogue record for this book is available from the British Library

ISBN 9781529106886

Typeset in 10/14.5 pt Arial by Jouve UK, Milton Keynes
Project management by whitefox
Printed and bound in Great Britain by Clays Ltd, Elcograf S.p.A.

MIX
Paper from
responsible sources
FSC
www.fsc.org
FSC® C018179

Penguin Random House is committed to a
sustainable future for our business, our readers and
our planet. This book is made from Forest
Stewardship Council® certified paper.

Contents

INTRODUCTION ⟫ 1

INDOOR GAMES ⟫ 5
Games Involving Household Items 8
Dice/Coin Games 33
Card Games 50
Pencil-and-Paper Games 87

OUTDOOR GAMES ⟫ 117
Ball Games 120
Other Equipment 136

TRAVEL GAMES ⟫ 147
Word Games 150
Looking Out the Window Games 194
Hand Games 214

HOLIDAY GAMES ⟫ 223
Swimming Pool Games 226
Beach Games 244

PARTY AND BIG GROUP GAMES ⟫ 255
Big Group/Playground 258
Party Games 281

Index ⟫ 419

Useful Tips ⟫ 425

Acknowledgements ⟫ 426

Introduction

Holidays are different as a grown-up. Six weeks off school is amazing as a kid, while for most adults it is at best an admin nightmare and at worst a never-ending span of time to try and keep your offspring vaguely occupied without going mad. It's easy to find yourself fried, frazzled, drawing a total blank and feeling like term time can't come soon enough, and that's not what holidays are about.

Add the ridiculous allure of electronics everywhere and it gets even worse. How can you compete with an infinite selection of bonkers-looking cartoons, violent video games and live-streams of teenage millionaires talking about bonkers-looking cartoons and violent video games?

Sometimes, the answer might be 'with some balled-up socks and a laundry basket'.

There are five hundred games in this book, few of which require anything more complicated than a ball, stationery or the occasional smelly sock. If you've got an amazing supply of specialist equipment, great, but there are plenty of options in here that require next to nothing. There is also a 501st game snaking its way through the whole thing, a 52-game-long trail weaving back and forth – at one a week, that's a year's worth of screen-free fun. And, if unsure what you want to do, there are Find Some Fun flow charts to help you decide.

There are word games, memory games, drinking games with the drinking removed and Victorian parlour games that have been dragged into the twenty-first century. There are ancient Chinese games, medieval European games, games with sneaky maths in and games that have had the word 'laser' added to them to make them sound more interesting.

The idea is that this book is just there if you need it: a useful thing to keep in the bookcase or glove compartment, knowing that if, for instance, outdoor plans are scuppered by rain, you have options beyond staring at phones and arguing. Ideally, this book will end up dog-eared and sun-bleached, filled with scrawled additions, annotations and score tallies. In a true crisis it can also be used as a bat.

Smartphones are fun and all, but a lot more treasured memories are made by, say, hitting a tennis ball with a frying pan. It might not be the best hit ever, and it might not do much for the frying pan, but in the right circumstances it could lead to the most fun anyone's ever had.

The book is divided into six categories, in roughly ascending order of age/difficulty within each one:

INDOOR GAMES can, firstly, be played regardless of weather. They include pencil-and-paper games, card games and anything involving basic household items. From incredibly basic games involving scrawling a few lines to DIY hallway bowling alleys, find them here.

OUTDOOR GAMES involve being outside in a garden or park but don't require huge numbers of people.

TRAVEL GAMES need minimal equipment and can be played in the back seat of a car. Some require looking out of the window at the world going by, but a lot just require a bit of imagination. Crucially, none require Baby Shark being blasted for the hundredth time.

HOLIDAY GAMES involve being in places like swimming pools and the beach – if you have access to these all the time, you can disregard the holiday part.

PARTY GAMES are those that can keep lots of children entertained but require someone taking on something of a ringmaster role. Some require a bit more preparation and gathering together of bits and bobs.

BIG GROUP GAMES are for big groups of kids to go off and play on their own. (Adult supervision is still advisable.)

Everything in this book is just a suggestion, a starting point to be moulded to whatever your situation. Play indoor games outside, play four-player games with forty people. Add rules, change rules, ignore rules, and modify any and all elements around your own particular requirements. Do whatever you want, and enjoy!

Indoor Games

Find Some Fun: At Home

Use this high-tech, futuristic method to find a game to play, because why should you have to do all the work yourself?

Would making a big mess be a bad idea?

Yes

No

Do you have a pack of cards handy?

Try DIY Bowling [14], you can do untold damage to a hallway.

Yes

No

Give Spit [82] or Beggar My Neighbour [59] a go.

Right then. You thinking of going outside?

No

Do you have a ball?

Stuck in the Mud [263] or British Bulldog [270]: no stuff, just lots of running around. Fun!

Yes

Yes

Give Eliminate [121] or Horse [127] a go.

Are there lots of you?

No

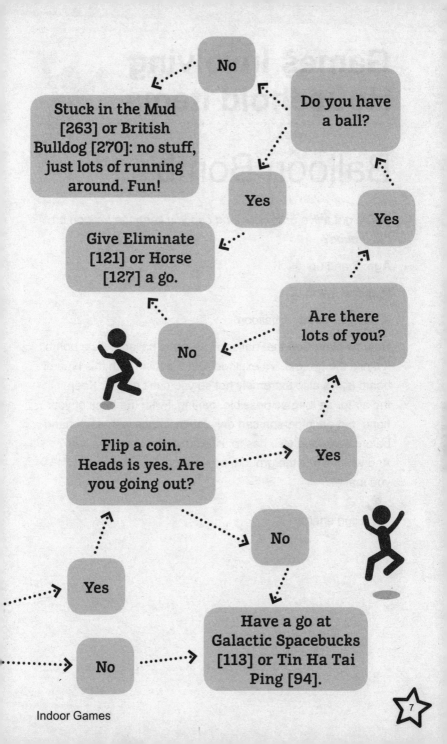

Flip a coin. Heads is yes. Are you going out?

Yes

Yes

No

No

Have a go at Galactic Spacebucks [113] or Tin Ha Tai Ping [94].

Games Involving Household Items

Balloon Bomb

We've got a live one! How long can you keep the balloon off the ground?

Age: 3 and up

Players: 2 and up

What you need: A balloon

How to play: See that balloon? It's not a balloon, it's a bomb. If it hits the ground, it'll explode. But the thing with this type of bomb is, it's also extremely hot so you can't grab it. Keep it in the air for as long as possible, batting it with the back of your hand, but each person can only touch it once with each hand before someone else has to. How long can you keep it up? And when it hits the ground, how loud a 'BOOM!' can you make?

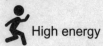 High energy

Hunt the Thimble

What even is *a thimble?*

Age: 3 and up

Players: 2 and up

What you need: Something small and distinctive

How to play: Look, nobody has thimbles any more. We live in the future. Instead, just use anything distinctive, unmistakable and small. A LEGO figure works perfectly. Either banish everyone from the room in order to hide it, or do so beforehand. Time to turn the place upside down looking for it!

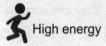 High energy

Big Game Thimble Hunting

A team version of Hunt The Thimble. Split into two teams. One team leaves the room/area for 2 minutes while the other works together to come up with the best possible hiding place for the figure/thing (again, nobody owns thimbles outside of fairy tales). When the hunters re-enter the room, the timer begins. Both teams have a go, and whoever finds it quickest wins.

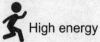 High energy

Beasts in the Tundra

A bit of preparation the night before and everyone becomes an archaeologist

Age: 4 and up

Players: 2 and up (dependent on freezer space)

What you need: One plastic box and one toy per player or team, a freezer

How to play: Freeze the toys in water in the plastic boxes the night before. Action figures or dinosaurs are ideal, and you can consider adding food colouring to the water to make it that bit wackier. Players then have to release their creatures from their frozen slumbers – just like Captain America – before their opponents. Breathing heavily onto the ice, rubbing it or wrapping it up might all work, or (with adult supervision) heat and gravity can work wonders . . .

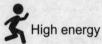 High energy

The Floor is Lava

Volcano!

Age: 4 and up

Players: 2 and up

What you need: Nothing, and yet somehow everything

How to play: Not so much a game as a sudden transition to a new way of life, The Floor Is Lava is a declaration that the floor has, in fact, been replaced by deathly molten magma, and contact with it is lethal. However – what are the odds? – the furniture has a kind of acid on it that starts to kill you if you stay still, so you need to keep moving around the room/house without touching the floor (although tactical use of rugs is permissible). The winner is the last person who remains unlava-ed.

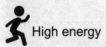 High energy

501 *Use those jumping skills in an adversarial manner in Piggy-in-the-Middle [120].*

The Floor is Lava ... and the Lava has Monsters

The only thing that could possibly exacerbate a situation where the floor has been replaced by lava: one where the floor has been replaced by monster-filled, transformative lava. As soon as anyone touches the floor, they become a lava monster and have to try to recruit everyone else to the hot side, whether by moving furniture to make it harder to remain out of the lava, standing in the way of jumps from one sofa to another – anything short of actively attacking one another.

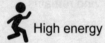 High energy

Hot and Cold

Using temperature as a metaphor for being really great at looking for things

Age: 4 and up

Players: 2 and up

What you need: Something small enough to hide

How to play: One player leaves the room for a few minutes while the secret object is hidden. When they come back to look for it, use temperature as a cue to direct them where to look: the nearer the object they are, the hotter everything gets. Don't just say 'hot' and 'cold', though – be as descriptive and dramatic as you can. 'As inhospitably sub-zero as the surface of Pluto', for instance. 'As cold as a penguin's swimming trunks.' 'Warmer than a sunbed on fire.' 'As hot as a kettle filled with curry at the centre of the Earth.'

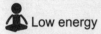 Low energy

501 *Speaking of cold, who wants some cold hard cash? Play Spin-the-Sovereign [43] for fame and fortune.*

DIY Bowling

Improvising your way into having a bowling alley is straightforward enough, and loads of fun

Age: 4 and up

Players: 2 and up

What you need: A ball, pen and paper, plus whatever is around – plastic bottles are ideal, but lots of things work. Aerosols of air freshener from the bathroom, empty cans, action figures, those things the kitchen roll rests on . . .

How to play: On a flat area, position 'skittles' in a triangle at one end (hallways are good for this) and take it in turns 'bowling' at them, keeping score on paper. You might decide certain skittles are worth more for being harder to knock over, or there are bonuses for knocking everything down. Experiment with different rules, and have fun!

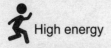 High energy

Professional DIY Bowling

Even if playing with washing-up liquid bottles and Christmas decorations, you can choose to use the proper bowling rules – ten skittles, ten frames, maximum of two rolls per frame, 1 point per skittle dropped. A spare (all skittles felled in two balls) scores 10 plus however many skittles are knocked down by the next ball, while a strike (all skittles knocked down in one go) is 10 plus however many are felled by the next two.

Each player has up to two rolls per turn (or 'frame') to knock down as many skittles as they can. If they knock down everything in one roll, that's a strike, scoring them 10 points plus the number they knock down on their next two balls. Knocking everything down with both rolls is a spare – 10 points plus whatever you get on your next roll. For instance, if Dave knocks everything down on his first turn, and then when it's his go again, knocks down three and then four, he finishes his second frame on a score of 24 – frame one scoring 17 (10 + 3 + 4) and frame two scoring 7. If you get a strike or a spare on the tenth frame, stand the pins up again for the extra roll or two. (Seems complicated? Blame the nineteenth-century enthusiasts who came up with bowling's annoying rules.)

 Low energy

Obstacle Course

Transform your house into an SAS-style training zone

Age: 5 and up

Players: 1 and up

What you need: Anything/everything you can find

How to play: Use your imagination and whatever you can find to turn your house into an obstacle course. Crawl under blankets! Vault over the back of the sofa! Jump over suitcases! Make stepping stones out of cushions! The fun is in coming up with new ideas and trying them out, but if you want a competitive element, a few of you can time each other going round as quickly as possible.

 High energy

Blindfolded Obstacle Course

Either do this one at a time (after doing the course without a blindfold enough times that you know it, and with supervision to prevent accidents), or in pairs with a non-blindfolded 'spotter' giving the blindfolded person directions.

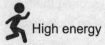 High energy

Blow Football

A huffing, puffing, indoor version of the world's most popular sport

Age: 5 and up

Players: 2

What you need: Two straws, a ping-pong ball and something for goals – margarine tubs, books, whatever works

How to play: Mark out a pitch (or use something that already ends – a rug or a table) using tape if needed, work out where the centre line is, and go for it, trying to score goals against your opponent. If anyone touches the ball with their hands, the other player gets a penalty from the centre line. The first to five goals wins.

 High energy

Blow Skiing

Make a slalom course around a table using whatever is to hand – clumps of Blu-Tack with toothpicks sticking up out of them and a little paper flag make very nice ski gates, for instance. Take it in turns to do time trials around the course, with a ten-second penalty for every flag hit and a 30-second penalty if the ball falls off the table.

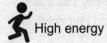 High energy

Scavenger Hunt

Bring age-old hunter-gatherer techniques perfected in prehistoric times to a more modern setting: your house

Age: 5 and up

Players: 2 and up

What you need: Paper and something to write with

How to play: Present players with a list of things to gather together from around the house – say, a pillow case, a toothbrush, three pencils of different colours, a clothes peg, a cuddly toy and a coin. Whoever gathers everything first wins. You can set extra rules, like only allowing them to carry one thing at once, or requiring them to be collected in strict order.

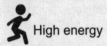 High energy

The Thoughtful Scavenger

Instead of going specific on your list, make it all a bit more esoteric and open to interpretation. Request something that rotates, something blue, something edible, something loved, something that starts with B. Get insights into your child's psyche by asking for something that means a lot to them, or treat yourself by demanding/requesting 'something I would find delicious'.

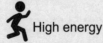 High energy

Teeny-Tiny Treasure Trove

The world's smallest scavenger hunt

Age: 5 and up

Players: 2 and up

What you need: Paper, pens, envelopes

How to play: Like a regular scavenger hunt, but everything is teeny-tiny, and the whole lot can fit in an envelope. Can you source a hair, a blade of grass, the smallest sock in the house? One piece of cereal, the tiniest pebble you can find, a microscopic breadcrumb? No cutting bits off clothes!
Whoever gets everything the tiniest wins – you could even get the kitchen scales out and weigh them if you can.

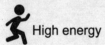 High energy

Show-Off Scavengers

Part scavenger hunt, part auction, as players have to pit their quickly sourced finds (gathered together within a strict time limit) against one another. Sure, you've all sourced a pen, but can you provide a compelling argument as to why the particular one you got is the best? One person – a millionaire – listens and decides which is best, and the scavenger who 'sells' the most to them wins.

 High energy

Laundry-Basket Horse

All the fun of basketball with the added element of smelly socks

Age: 5 and up

Players: 2 and up

What you need: Balled-up socks and a laundry basket (or beanbags and a saucepan/bucket/bin/bowl/anything), pen and paper to keep track of letters

How to play: The first player throws the 'ball' into the basket. If they miss, and player two stands in the same spot and makes the shot, player one gets a letter – the object of the game is to avoid getting all the letters of the word HORSE. If they make the shot, player two has to try and match it, or *they* get an H. Then it's player two's turn to do the first shot, from a new location. Keep trying to match each other's abilities until one player gets all the letters of the word HORSE.

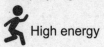 High energy

The Great Sock Hunt

A scavenger hunt that makes up in ease what it lacks in glamour

Age: 5 and up

Players: 2 and up

What you need: As many different pairs of socks as you wish

How to play: Hide one sock from every pair around the house, then present players with a pile of odd socks. Within a time limit (which depends on how big the house is, how many socks you've hidden, how good at hiding socks you are, and how good at finding socks they are – start with 5 minutes and experiment), and never carrying more than one sock at a time, can they reunite all the pairs?

 High energy

501 *Put those socks to work by making them into tails, with Cats-and-Mice [296].*

Super Secret 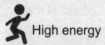 Sock Search

Hide the odd socks apart from one, which, instead of being hidden somewhere around the house, goes in your pocket. Players take it in turns to spend 1 minute each searching for socks, with each one they find eliminating one option as to what your pocketed Secret Sock could be. The player who correctly describes that sock wins.

High energy

Pick-up Pasta

A tactical spaghetti challenge

Age: 5 and up

Players: 2 and up

What you need: Uncooked spaghetti

How to play: Dump the spaghetti on the table so it is in a big jumbled mess, all criss-crossing and everywhere. Then, players take it in turns to pick up one piece at a time without moving any others. As soon as a piece of spaghetti other than the one the player is touching moves, their turn is over with no pasta acquired. Whoever has the most at the end of the game wins.

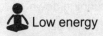 Low energy

> **501** *Don't let that spaghetti go to waste. Boil it up for a daft game of Sweetie in a Haystack [305].*

Non-stop Pick-up Pasta

When dumping the spaghetti out, pick up any loose bits that aren't touching any others and put them on top of the pile. Players' turns then last for as long (and as many pieces of spaghetti) as they can, but they have to keep moving at all times – there's no time to stop, ponder and plan. As soon as they move a piece other than the one they're extracting, their turn is over.

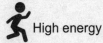 High energy

Racin' Riches, Rollin' Ramps

How far can you roll your precious wheel of gold?

Age: 6 and up

Players: 2

What you need: A £2 coin each, a ruler, a few books

How to play: Play in a long hallway or as big a room as possible. Set a teeing-off point and an end zone past a certain line. The aim is to get your coin from the teeing-off point to the end zone in as few rolls as possible. Use the stacked books and the ruler to make a ramp running down onto the floor, and tee off from the same spot. Then do subsequent shots by positioning the bottom of the ramp where the coin previously fell. Golf-scoring rules apply: lowest wins.

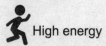 High energy

501 *Put that ruler to solid work with Battleship [89].*

Can Clatter

An extra-noisy game to play on resilient flooring

Age: 6 and up

Players: 2 and up

What you need: A ball, canned goods from the kitchen

How to play: Build a tower of cans at one end of a hallway with a floor that is unlikely to be damaged. Ten cans is plenty, in rows of four, three, two and one, although you can add a base row of five at the bottom if you have enough cans. Take it in turns throwing the ball at the cans and trying to knock as many down as possible.

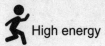 High energy

Snow Blower

Use your lungs to outdo one another

Age: 6 and up

Players: 2 and up

What you need: Cotton wool balls, straws

How to play: Start with a cotton wool ball each at one end of a smooth table. At the signal, race them to the other end just by blowing them using a straw. Longer courses can be built in houses with laminate flooring.

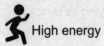 High energy

Catch My Drift

Start with five cotton wool balls each. Do you do them one at a time so you can really focus, or move each one a short distance with each blow then catch up? Thinking tactically might be the difference between glorious snowy victory and (metaphorically) melting into a sad puddle.

 High energy

Five Pence Hockey

Air hockey tables cost a fortune. This alternative costs less than anything.

Age: 7 and up

Players: 2

What you need: A table, tape, two 2p pieces, one 1p piece

How to play: Don't play on a table that is likely to get scratched – that'll make the game a lot more expensive. Use the tape to mark out equally sized goals. Then, stand one at either end and play hockey – slide your 2p around with your middle finger, using the penny as a puck. First to ten goals wins.

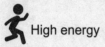 High energy

Ball Blow-off

An epic battle of lung vs lung

Age: 7 and up

Players: 4 and up

What you need: One ping-pong ball, a straw each, a table

How to play: Split into two teams, each along one side of the table. When the ball is dropped in the middle, the aim of the game is to blow it off the other side of the table while preventing the opposing team blowing it off your side. You can't touch the table with any part of your body, and are only allowed to blow the ball with your straw – no touching or hitting it.

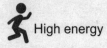 High energy

Paper Rugby

Much more indoorsy than the regular kind

Age: 8 and up

Players: 2

What you need: One piece of A4 paper, a smooth table to play on

How to play: First, fold the paper into your 'ball' – fold it twice lengthways to make a strip, then fold the top corner down to make a triangular flap. Fold the flap over itself as many times as you can, and tuck the final flap into the fold – that's your rugby ball. Players sit either side of a table and attempt to score 'a try' – ending up with the ball sticking off the table on their opponent's side without falling off onto the floor. They do this by flicking it, starting from their own end, with a maximum of four flicks. If no try is scored, the ball is turned over to the other player. If a try is scored, there is the chance to convert: posts are made by the scored-upon player forming L-shapes with their fingers and thumbs and putting their thumbs together on the table – one flick from the centre of the table through the posts converts. A try scores 5, a conversion 2. Play for 10 minutes, with the highest-scoring player winning.

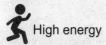 High energy

501 *For a much rougher version of this that still involves stationery, give Chalk Rugby [418] a go.*

Sock Wrestling

Smelly, smelly roughhousing

Age: 8 and up

Players: 2 and up

What you need: A soft surface to play on

How to play: Players remove their shoes and try to pull one another's socks off. The first player to be rendered barefoot loses – it's as simple as that. Some bouts last seconds, some result in hour-long grapples (not many). With more than two players, a straightforward tournament structure is easy enough to figure out to eventually crown the Stinky Champion.

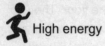 High energy

Metre Made

A game of guessing, estimating and guesstimating

Age: 8 and up

Players: 2 and up

What you need: A pencil and ruler or tape measure, plus a chair or stool to stand on

How to play: Can you make a mark on the wall exactly a metre up without using a tape measure? What about 48.4cm, the height of Arcturus, the world's tallest cat? Or 90cm, the height of a dodo? Get 1 point for every centimetre you are off by, and the lowest score wins.

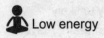 Low energy

Hallway Curling

Bring the Winter Olympics' most oddly compelling event to life in a corridor with laminate flooring

Age: 8 and up

Players: 2 and up

What you need: Two unopened bars of soap, a soft broom, tape

How to play: Play on laminate flooring with tape you are 100% certain won't ruin everything. Mark out two concentric circles with tape – the centre about 15cm in diameter, the outer circle 50cm. Following proper curling rules you'd have eight bars of soap each, but that seems highly unlikely (nobody is that clean), so instead have one per team. Player one slides their soap (or, in curling parlance, 'stone') along the floor, aiming to get it to stop as close to the centre circle ('the button') as possible. Player two then slides theirs, free to knock player one's out of the way. Whoever ends up nearest the button wins the point, with 2 bonus points if they end up actually within it, and 1 for ending up within the outer circle. Both players can, if they really want to, use a soft broom to sweep in front of a sliding stone to affect where it goes, as long as they are willing to accept it might not actually help in any way. First to 11 points wins.

 Low energy

Dice/Coin Games

Three Heads and Three Tails

Laws of probability mean this game can theoretically last forever

Age: 5 and up

Players: 2

What you need: A coin, plus six additional pennies or counters for lives, or pen and paper

How to play: Start with three lives each. Take it in turns to flip a coin ten times. Any time you get three heads or three tails in a row, take a life from your opponent. The winner is the last player left alive.

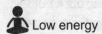 Low energy

Fifty-Headed Monster

Take it in turns to do five flips each, keeping a tally of your results, and the first to reach 50 heads wins.

Dice Mountain

Who can be first to descend the other side of the mountain?

Age: 5 and up

Players: 2 to 4

What you need: Two dice, pencil and paper, coloured pencils (optional)

How to play: Graph paper or squared paper is great for this, as it lets you draw a really brilliant-looking mountain with a nice plateau on top. If not, just draw a mountain each with the numbers 1, 2, 3, 4, 5, 6, 6, 6, 5, 4, 3, 2, 1 going up one slope, across the top and down the other side. Throw both dice at once and cross off the numbers or colour in as much of the mountain as you can – however, you can only do one section of slope at a time, i.e. a 2 is no use if you haven't had a 1 yet when beginning your ascent, just as all the 4s in the world are useless to you when stuck on the plateau of 6s, but if both dice are useful (say, you throw a 1 and a 2 together), you can do two sections at once. The first to successfully climb the mountain, cross the plateau and fully descend is the winner.

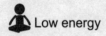 Low energy

Dice Himalaya

Use three dice, with a mountain that is 12 high and has a jagged plateau: 1, 2, 3, 4, 5, 6, 7, 8, 9, 10, 11, 12, 11, 12, 11, 12, 11, 12, 11, 12, 11, 10, 9, 8, 7, 6, 5, 4, 3, 2, 1. On every throw, two or three dice can be combined if necessary to make higher numbers.

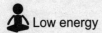 Low energy

54321

A quick, straightforward game of throwing and dying

Age: 6 and up

Players: 2 to 4

What you need: Five dice, plus three pennies or counters per player for lives

How to play: Everyone starts with three lives. In one turn, a player throws five dice, then re-throws four, then three, then two, then one. The aim is to end up with the lowest score after your five throws – when everyone has had their turn, the person with the highest number after all five hands a life over to the person with the lowest. Players are out when they lose all their lives.

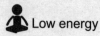 Low energy

Ship, Captain and Crew

Can you sail the seven seas with a full ship?

Age: 6 and up

Players: 2 to 4

What you need: Five dice, plus three pennies or counters per player for lives

How to play: Start with three lives each. Every player aims to set sail with a ship (a six), a captain (a five), a crew (a four) and cargo (the other two dice), and has three throws to get what they need. After each throw, players can save any dice they wish to keep, rather than rethrowing all five, but can only do so in order – you can't have a captain without a ship, a crew without a captain or cargo without a crew. After three throws, players who get their ship, captain and crew score however many spots are on their cargo, while players who don't manage score 0. The lowest scorer(s) lose a life, and the last sailor standing wins.

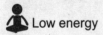 Low energy

Macau

A quickfire game of knowing when to stop

Age: 6 and up

Players: 2 to 4

What you need: One dice, one cup and three pennies or counters each for lives

How to play: The aim of the game is to score exactly 9 and no higher – scoring higher than 9 means you've gone bust and have nothing. Players take it in turns to throw the dice as many times as necessary, deciding when to play it safe and stick where they are rather than throwing again and risking going bust. At the end of the round, whoever scored exactly 9 – or, if nobody did, whoever came closest – takes a life from everyone else. Paying attention to how the players before you have done is really helpful – if you are going last and everyone has gone bust, for instance, you can throw anything at all, stick and win.

 Low energy

Fünfzehn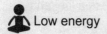

The same rules as Macau, but with fifteen (or, in German, *fünfzehn*) as the score everyone is aiming for. One extra rule: if anyone manages to throw seven times without going bust, they win.

 Low energy

Liars' Dice

Popularly played at Chinese New Year, this game requires a bit of maths and a lot of dice

Age: 8 and up

Players: 2 to 5

What you need: Five dice and an opaque cup per player, plus three pennies or counters per player for lives

How to play: Everyone starts with three lives, a cup and five dice. Roll one dice each to see who goes first (highest wins). Then all players shake their dice in their cup and slam them down on the table, taking a peek but keeping them hidden from everyone else. The first player makes a guess as to how many of a certain dice value might be on the table, including everyone's dice – 'two fours', for instance. The rest of the players then get a chance to either accept that and move on, or call it a lie. If they accept it, the next player has to make a guess that involves at least one more dice and a higher spot total – in this case, three fives would be acceptable but four twos wouldn't – and so on. After anyone's prediction, another player can call them a liar, at which point everyone lifts their cup to reveal their dice. If the named dice are present, the accuser gives the accused one of their lives, and vice versa. The winner then starts the next round.

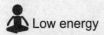 Low energy

501 *Digging this? Try another great Chinese game, the hands-only Hoi Sai [219].*

A Pair of Liars

You only need two dice and one cup for this variation. Player one shakes the dice in the cup, slams it down and peeks, then gives the result as a two-digit number – the higher dice first, the lower second, so a one and a five would be 51. The other players can accept this and move on, in which case play continues to player two, or accuse player one of lying. When an accusation of lying is made, the cup is lifted and the real result revealed. If no accusation is made, the next player can shake and slam their dice up to three times before stating their number, which must be higher than the one before.

 Low energy

Sevens, Elevens and Doubles

Very few rules, no skill required

Age: 6 and up

Players: 2 to 6

What you need: Two dice, plus five pennies or counters per player for lives

How to play: Everyone starts with five lives. Take it in turns to roll the dice. If you get anything other than a seven, an eleven or a double, put one of your lives in the middle of the table. If you roll a seven, an eleven or any double, take all the lives that are on the table. Play until only one player has any lives left.

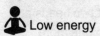 Low energy

Five Coins and a Cup

There's money involved, but everyone leaves with the same bank balance they showed up with

Age: 7 and up

Players: 2 to 4

What you need: Five coins, a cup, plus 20 pennies or counters per player for lives, or pen and paper

How to play: Each player starts with 20 lives. One player shakes all the coins in the cup and dumps them on the table, shouting 'heads' or 'tails' as they do so. Each coin that shows the other side puts one life in danger, but if the player wants, they can go double or nothing on one more flip of one coin. For instance, if you shout 'tails' and dump out two heads and three tails, you can either lose two lives or flip one more coin – call it correctly and you keep all your lives, or get it wrong and lose four. Take it in turns until there is only one player remaining alive.

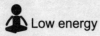 Low energy

Spin the Sovereign

A game of dexterity, precision and cold hard cash

Age: 7 and up

Players: 2 to 4

What you need: A round coin – a 10p or £2 is ideal – and a flat surface like a coffee table, plus three pennies or counters per player for lives

How to play: Everyone starts with three lives. One player spins the coin on its side and (if playing with more than two players) calls out another player's name. The called player must either stop the coin upright with their finger (in which case the first player loses a life) or give it another flick to keep it spinning and call another player's name, who then has the same options. Trying to stop the coin upright but knocking it over costs you a life, as does spinning it off the table or doing such a rubbish spin that it just falls over. Play until only one player remains alive.

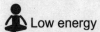 Low energy

501 *Combine money and gravity with Racin' Riches, Rollin' Ramps [24].*

43

Pig

Beloved of maths teachers everywhere, but don't let that put you off

Age: 7 and up

Players: 2 and up

What you need: A dice, paper and pen

How to play: Players take it in turns rolling the dice as many times as they like to amass as many points as possible, aiming to reach 100. However, if they roll a one, they lose all their points for that turn and their turn ends. Are you better off banking your points or keeping going and risking losing them all?

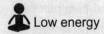 Low energy

> **501** *If you like the dice but aren't so keen on the maths, try Dice, Dice, Very Nice [285].*

A Pair of Pigs

The same rules as standard Pig, but played with two dice and additional rules: if you throw a pair of ones, your entire score (not just that turn) reverts to 0, and if you throw any other pair, you have to roll again and aren't allowed to bank your points.

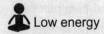 Low energy

Shift Right

A simple-looking but really tactical game that involves thinking multiple moves ahead

Age: 8 and up

Players: 2

What you need: Pen and paper, three to five coins

How to play: Draw a row of between 10 and 20 squares big enough to contain a coin. Put the coins in whatever squares you wish. Players sit next to one another and take it in turns to move one coin one, two or three squares to the right. Multiple coins sharing a space is not allowed, and nor is jumping one coin over another. One player wins when the other has no moves left. Experiment with different lengths of board and different numbers of coins.

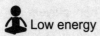 Low energy

Chickenfoot

Suitable for vegans, despite the name

Age: 8 and up

Players: 2 to 4

What you need: Dominoes

How to play: Scatter the dominoes face down, and select five each. If anyone has the double six, they start – if nobody has it, whoever has the double five, and if nobody has that, the double four and so on. (If nobody has a double, put your dominoes back and start again.) If it's the double six, the next player plays any six they have, coming off that domino either straight out of it or at a right angle – there are four directions that tiles with sixes on can come out of it. Keep going from player to player until all four of those have sixes on, with players drawing another tile if they can't go. Then, players continue adding a tile to play in whatever direction they can. If they can't go, they draw a tile, but can play it immediately if it is valid. When someone plays a double, they call out 'Chickenfoot!' and the focus shifts to putting three dominoes coming off that one – one straight forward and one each at 45 degrees to either side. Play continues until one person runs out of tiles or nobody can make a move. Players score 1 point for every spot left in their hand. Play six rounds, starting the second with the double five and so on, and at the end the player with the lowest score wins.

 Low energy

Mia

Dice, deception and doubling down

Age: 8 and up

Players: 3 or more

What you need: Two dice, one opaque cup and a way of recording lives – paper, six pennies per player, or even another dice each

How to play: Everyone starts with six lives – one option is to use a spare dice each to keep track. The first player shakes the two dice in play in the cup, turns it over onto the table and has a peek before either announcing the actual number of spots shown or opting to lie and just make a number up. The next player can either roll again, in which case they have to announce a higher number of spots regardless of what they actually roll, or they can accuse the first player of lying. (If the player before you has said 12, you might as well accuse them of lying, because nobody is going to believe you rolled 13.) If they do this, the cup is lifted and the dice revealed – if fewer dots are showing than were stated, player one loses a life and player two starts a new round. But if the dots showing are equal to or greater than the number stated, player two loses a life and player three starts the next round. The last player alive wins.

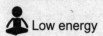 Low energy

Dice 101

A low-fi, non-sharp darts spinoff

Age: 9 and up

Players: 2

What you need: Five dice, pen and paper

How to play: Both players start with 101 points, and are aiming to reach exactly 0 before their opponent. They take it in turns to throw between one and five dice, taking the total dots shown off their points (a maximum of 30 per throw). You can't go into negative numbers, so a throw that would take you below zero (for instance, being on 18 and throwing three fives, a six and a four) is completely forfeit – as your score dwindles, you need to choose when to throw fewer dice.

 Low energy

Dice 404

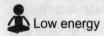

An advanced variation on Dice 101. Each player draws four columns on their paper, each starting on 101. They then play as normal, but with every turn they can choose which column to take the score off. The winner is the first player to take three of their four columns down to 0.

 Low energy

Yacht

Five dice, 12 chances, no going back

Age: 9 and up

Players: 2 and up

What you need: Five dice, pen and paper

How to play: Yacht works by players throwing five dice up to three times, keeping some after each throw if they wish and using the end result on their scorecard in one of 12 categories – after every turn, a score has to be recorded on their scorecard, even if it's 0. Before playing, each player draws themselves a scorecard with 12 categories: One to Six (each of which score the total number of dots of that number shown – i.e. in the fours category, a roll of two fours, two sixes and a three would score 8), Full House (two of one number, three of another, scoring the total dots shown), Four of a Kind (scoring the total of those four dice, i.e. 16 for four fours), Low Straight (one to five, scoring 30), High Straight (two to six, also scoring 30), Freestyle (scoring however many dots are showing) and Yacht (five of a kind, scoring 50). Once written down, scores are final – for instance, if you've put 0 in the Yacht category and then you roll five ones, you might have to put it in Ones and only score five points for it. If you've already put a 0 in the High Straight category but then roll a High Straight, well, that's just rotten luck. After 12 hands and full scorecards, the highest score wins.

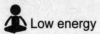 Low energy

Card Games

Skirmish

A straightforward game of luck and shouting

Age: 5 and up

Players: 2

What you need: A deck of cards

How to play: Deal the cards between both players, who hold their piles face down. Players take it in turns to go 'One, two, three, BANG!', with both of them turning over their top card on the bang. Whoever has the higher card (aces are highest, twos lowest) takes them both and adds them to the bottom of their pile. If both cards are of the same value, each player has to deploy their extra weapon by counting out three cards face down, turning over a fourth and playing that. The winner gets all the cards in the middle (or, if it is a draw again, another four cards are deployed each). Keep playing until one player has all the cards.

 Low energy

Global Skirmish

A variant for three or four players. Deal all the cards and play as normal, taking it in turns to count to a bang and place a card down. However, this time, if the highest card is a draw, each player deploys only two cards as their extra weapon. The winner gets all the cards in the middle.

 Low energy

Memory

Half luck, half skill, all infuriating

Age: 5 and up

Players: 2 to 4

What you need: A deck of cards

How to play: Play with only the red cards. Lay them out face down in a grid, either in two rows of thirteen or two rows of six and two of seven. Take it in turns turning two cards over, looking for pairs. If you find a pair, you keep them. If not, you put the cards back. Pay attention to what everyone else is turning over – that's how you end up getting pairs. When all the pairs have been found, the player with the most wins.

 Low energy

Memory Deluxe

The same as standard Memory, but using a full deck of cards (four rows of thirteen or four of six and four of seven), and looking for coloured pairs – i.e., the two red sevens or the two black threes. It's double the cards but requires approximately quintuple the memory skills.

 Low energy

Snip Snap Snorem

An old-school German game from the eighteenth century

Age: 5 and up

Players: 2 to 4

What you need: A deck of cards

How to play: Deal out all the cards (or, with three players, all but one card so everyone has the same amount, or with five players, all but two). The player to the left of the dealer starts by placing any card down, announcing its rank (e.g., 'Queen!'). The next player then matches it if they can with a card of the same rank, saying 'Snip!' The next, if they also have a queen, places it down saying 'Snap!', and if the next player has the final queen, they play it, saying 'Snorem!' However, if it is your turn and you don't have a matching card, you don't get to put anything down – the player who put the last matching card down begins another round. The winner is the first to get rid of all of their cards.

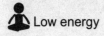 Low energy

Schnipp Schnapp Schnorem

Play works in the same way, but with the added element of lives – everyone starts out with ten pennies or counters, and at the end of each round gives the winner one life for every card they have left. Keep going until only one player remains alive.

 Low energy

Snap

Intensely competitive, pleasantly straightforward and delightfully loud

Age: 5 and up

Players: 2 to 5

What you need: A deck of cards

How to play: Deal all the cards out. Each player holds their pile of cards, face down, and takes it in turns laying a card down, one on top of the other, face up. If two cards of the same number are put down in a row, the first player to shout 'Snap!' and slap their hand down on the pile gets all the cards in the pile. The object of the game is to get the whole pack. When you run out of cards you have one more chance to get the next snap, and if you miss it, you're out.

 Low energy

Slapjack

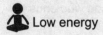

Like normal Snap, but instead of matching pairs you are looking for jacks (if removing any cards from the deck to make sure every player has the same amount of cards, make sure no jacks are taken). When someone places a jack on the pile, everyone tries to hit it and shout 'Slapjack!' The game ends when one player wins all the cards.

 Low energy

Irish Snap

A variation on traditional Snap with more public declarations

Age: 5 and up

Players: 2 to 5

What you need: A deck of cards

How to play: Deal all the cards out. Players hold them face down and take it in turns placing one face up in the middle, calling out a card rank as they do so – the first player says 'Ace', the second 'Two' and so on, starting again if you reach king. If a card is placed down that matches the rank called out, everyone shouts 'Snap!' and slams their hand on the pile. The last one to slam their hand down – or the person whose hand is on top of everyone else's – takes the whole pile and starts another round. The winner is the first person to get rid of all of their cards, while the loser is the person who ends up with the whole deck.

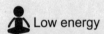 Low energy

501 *Go from Ireland to France with the help of a bat, with French Cricket [279].*

Silent Sevens

Normal Irish Snap rules apply, but once you get to seven, everyone stops saying the numbers out loud and has to keep track in their heads instead. If you get all the way to king, start again and get up to seven again, the silence ends and you start stating the numbers again.

 Low energy

Chase the Ace

Age: 5 and up

Players: 2 or more

What you need: A deck of cards, plus five pennies or counters per player as lives

How to play: Each player is dealt one card face down, and an extra card is dealt in the middle. Everyone begins with five lives. With aces high, the idea is to finish with the highest card you can. One by one, you can choose to keep your card or change it with the unknown card – watch your opponents' reactions when they swap for clues. When everyone has had a turn, the player with the lowest card loses a life. If two players have the same low card, they both lose a life. The cards are placed on the bottom of the pile, the pile is shuffled and a new hand is dealt. The last player alive wins.

 Low energy

Go Fish

Listening is key in this classic game

Age: 5 and up

Players: 3 and up

What you need: A deck of cards

How to play: Deal seven cards to each player, and spread the rest out on the table – this is the 'sea'. Take it in turns to ask any player for a card to match one you have – e.g. 'Toby, do you have a six?' If Toby has any sixes he has to hand them all over, and if not he says 'go fish' and you have to pick a card up from the sea. The aim is to collect sets of four (e.g., all the tens), which you then put down. The winner is the player with the most sets at the end.

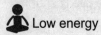 Low energy

One Fish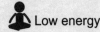

As above, but only one card changes hands at a time – rather than hand over all of their cards of the rank requested, only one is handed over. If you think they might have another one, you can ask again. Your turn finishes either when you want to, or when you get a negative response and have to pick up a fish.

 Low energy

Beggar My Neighbour

As played by Pip in Charles Dickens' Great Expectations, *literature fans*

Age: 6 and up

Players: 2 to 4

What you need: A deck of cards

How to play: Deal all the cards out. Players hold their cards in a pile, face down, then take it in turns to turn one over and place it on a pile in the middle. If a face card (jack, queen, king or ace) is placed down, the next player pays a 'penalty' – one card for a jack, two for a queen, three for a king and four for an ace. If no face cards are placed down during the penalty, the player who put the face card down gets to take the whole pile. If the penalty includes a face card, the next player has to pay the penalty appropriate to that one. The winner is the player who ends up with all the cards.

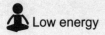 Low energy

Ratkiller

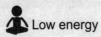

The same rules as Beggar My Neighbour, but with some of the elements of Snap as well. The same penalties apply for face cards, but any time two cards of the same value are played in a row, you can slap the pile, shout 'Ratkiller!' (or the vegetarian option, 'Ratkisser!') and win the pile of cards.

 Low energy

Old Maid

Who will be left with the elderly queen?

Age: 6 and up

Players: 2 to 4

What you need: A deck of cards

How to play: Remove the queen of clubs from the deck, and deal the rest out to everyone. Players look at their hands and take out any pairs they have, putting them on the table face up. If you have three of a kind, don't put them down. One player at a time then offers their cards to the person to their left, who takes one without looking. If it means they have a pair, they place the pair on the table (getting four of a kind is two pairs and also placed on the table). Play continues until one person is left with the solitary queen.

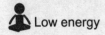 Low energy

Mystery Maid

Rather than removing the queen of clubs, the dealer shuffles the cards and takes the top one off, returning it to the box unseen so nobody knows what the unpairable card is. Pairs also have to be matched by colour – i.e., two red sevens rather than the seven of clubs and the seven of hearts counting as a pair. The player who ends up with one card left over loses.

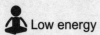 Low energy

Change

Age: 6 and up

Players: 2 and up

What you need: A deck of cards

How to play: Deal seven cards each, and turn over the top card of the remaining pile. The first player must put down a card of the same suit, or the same value and different suit – if this is the case, they say 'change', and play continues with this new suit. If a player can't go, they pick up cards from the draw pile one by one until a suitable card turns up. The winner is the first to get rid of all of their cards.

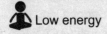 Low energy

Higher or Lower

Educated guesses and sheer dumb luck

Age: 6 and up

Players: 2 and up

What you need: A deck of cards, a pen and paper

How to play: Shuffle the cards and turn over the top one. One card at a time, the player decides whether the next card will be higher or lower than the one shown (aces are low). They score 1 point for every card they guess correctly, and can retire from the round at any point – if they get one wrong, they score 0 for that round. Play five rounds, shuffling the deck whenever you run out of cards. Highest score wins.

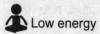 Low energy

Rolling Stone

A deeply frustrating card game, in which victory might seem inevitable then disappear in a heartbeat

Age: 6 and up

Players: 4 to 6

What you need: A deck of cards

How to play: Remove one set from the deck if playing with six people, three sets if playing with five, and five sets if playing with four, to give each player eight cards. Deal all the cards out, and give players time to arrange them by suit. The youngest player starts by playing any card, and going clockwise, everyone else has to play any card of the same suit on top of it. As soon as someone can't go, they have to take the whole discarded pile, and the player after them begins a new round. The player who ends up with the whole deck loses.

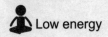 Low energy

My Ship Sails

A nautical game of card-collecting

Age: 6 and up

Players: 4 to 7

What you need: A deck of cards

How to play: Deal seven cards to each player and put the rest aside. The object of the game is to be the first to get seven cards of the same suit (although, depending on how many players you have, there might not actually be seven of each suit in play). Everyone looks at their cards and discards one, face down, onto the table to their right. Then, everyone picks up the discarded one to their left. Play continues like this until someone gets seven of the same suit, at which point they say 'My ship sails' and show them to everyone. If two players' ships sail at the same time, whoever says it first wins.

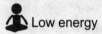 Low energy

Put Your Finger on Your Nose

Can you concentrate on both your cards and everyone's faces?

Age: 6 and up

Players: 5 to 12

What you need: A deck of cards, plus pennies or counters for lives

How to play: Sort the cards so you have three each of the same number of cards as players – i.e., if you have six players, you want eighteen cards, three each of ace to six. Every player starts with three lives. When the dealer shouts 'Go!', you slam one card down on the table to your left and pick up the one the person to your right has slammed down. When someone has three of a kind, they put their finger on their nose. The last person to notice what's happened and also put their finger on their nose. The winner is the last player left alive.

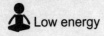 Low energy

Spoon Quest

Follow the rules of Put Your Finger On Your Nose, but have a pile of spoons in the middle of the table – one fewer than there are players. When you get three of a kind, grab a spoon, and the person who doesn't get a spoon loses a life. There's very little room for disagreements in this variation – either you have a spoon or you don't.

 Low energy

Uno

An internationally beloved classic, playable with a regular deck

Age: 7 and up

Players: 2 to 4

What you need: Two decks of cards shuffled together

How to play: Deal seven cards each, and place the rest of the cards face down as the draw pile. Players take it in turns placing cards down, matching either the suit or the number with the previously played card. Face cards have extra abilities, though: a jack skips the next player's turn, a queen means the next player has to draw two cards, a king means they have to draw four and an ace can be played on anything and changes the suit accordingly. If you can't play any of your cards, draw one from the pile. When the draw pile runs out, turn over the discard pile. When anyone is down to one card, they have to announce 'Uno!' – if they forget to announce this, and someone else challenges them on it, they have to draw a card. The winner is the first person to get rid of all of their cards.

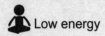 Low energy

24

Show off your mental arithmetic skills in a competitive way

Age: 7 and up

Players: 2 to 4

What you need: A deck of cards with the kings, queens and jacks removed

How to play: Deal four cards onto the table. The object of the game is to use the numbers shown to make a sum equalling the number 24, using addition, multiplication, subtraction and division. The first player to figure out a solution claps their hands and announces it. If it does come to 24, they win those cards. If not, another player can clap and try. If nobody can come up with a solution, the cards are shuffled back into the deck and four more dealt. When you've gone through the whole deck, whoever has the most cards wins.

 Low energy

24 Hours

A longer-lasting variant of 24. Play works in the same way, but you begin by dealing all of the cards out to players. Four cards are placed in the middle (two each with two players, one each with four players, and two cards from one player and one card each from the other two with three players, taking it in turns to be the one that puts two down). Whoever claps and gets the sum takes the cards. If there's no solution, another set of cards is dealt and whoever gets that one takes all eight cards. The winner is the player who ends up with the full deck.

 Low energy

Little Trumps

Nothing to do with anyone in the White House and everything to do with the cards in your hand

Age: 7 and up

Players: 2 to 5

What you need: A deck of cards

How to play: Seven cards are dealt to each player, and the remaining pile is then cut to reveal the 'trump' suit – i.e., if you cut the cards and reveal the five of hearts, hearts are trumps. The first player puts down any card, and the next has to put down a higher card of the same suit. If they don't have a higher card of the same suit, they draw a card from the pile, or play a card from the trump suit. Any trump, even a low one, beats any non-trump card, and only a higher trump can be played on it. If everyone has to pass and draw a card, whoever played the card they passed on goes again. The aim of the game is to get rid of all of your cards first.

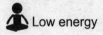 Low energy

Thirty-One

Age: 7 and up

Players: 4 or more

What you need: A deck of cards, plus three pennies or counters per person for lives

How to play: Everyone starts with three lives. Each player is dealt three cards, and another three are dealt in the middle of the table, face up. The aim for each player is to get the highest number of the same suit (the maximum possible being 31 – two tens/picture cards and an ace, with an ace counting as eleven). Taking it in turns, players can choose to swap either one or all three of their cards (but not two). When everyone has played, the winner is the player whose total is closest to 31. That player takes a life from everyone. Keep going until only one player remains.

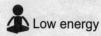 Low energy

Card Dominoes

This game comes with the added advantage of resulting in a neatly sorted deck

Age: 8 and up

Players: 2 to 5

What you need: A deck of cards

How to play: Deal all the cards out and give players a minute or so to sort them into order. Whoever has the seven of diamonds goes first, placing it down. Play continues to the left, where that player has the options, depending on their hand, of putting the eight of diamonds on top, the six of diamonds underneath, beginning a new pile with a different seven or passing. Play then continues with everyone taking turns to add a card to the top or bottom of a pile, passing or starting new ones as they go, with the winner the first to get rid of all their cards. When piling them up, it makes sense to stagger the pile a bit to show the ranks of all the cards in it.

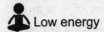 Low energy

Happy Families

Usually played with special decks involving alliterative names and occupations, but doable with a standard deck

Age: 8 and up

Players: 3 to 5

What you need: A deck of cards, but take out everything between two and six

How to play: The aim of the game is to complete the most families – each family being a set of four cards of the same rank. Deal out all of the cards – it doesn't matter if some players have more cards than others. If anyone has any complete families, lay them down. Players take it in turns to ask others for specific cards to help them complete sets, but in doing so, have to show at least one card they have in that set. For instance, asking 'Charlie, do you have the jack of spades?' while showing Charlie the jack of clubs. If the answer is yes, the card is handed over and they may ask another player for another card. If the answer is no, it is the next player's turn to ask someone for a card. Paying attention to what other people are asking for (and getting) is key here. When one player has no cards left, whoever has the most complete families is the winner.

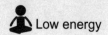 Low energy

Famous Families ......

Just to make things slightly trickier, instead of asking by suit, each suit is assigned a name as one of a group of four. You can use any group of four people – One Direction (post-Zayn, pre-hiatus), the Obamas, the members of the Simpson family that don't have dummies in their mouths, the Beatles, the Horsemen of the Apocalypse, your next-door neighbours – but everyone has to stick to it. Assign one name to clubs, one to spades, one to hearts and one to diamonds, and anyone who says the suit instead of the name (or gets it completely wrong, like 'Do you have the Ringo of clubs?') misses their turn.

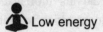 Low energy

Diplomat

Detective work is key, combining information available to everyone and things only you know about your hand

Age: 8 and up

Players: 3 to 6

What you need: A deck of cards

How to play: Deal out all the cards, and give everyone a minute to sort them out. If anyone has a full set of four, they say 'set' and put them down. When it is your turn, you can ask any other player for a card – 'Maddie, do you have a six?' – and if they have it, they hand it over. You can ask as many times as you want – if you think Maddie has three sixes, you can ask three times – until you get a no, at which point it is the next player's turn. Listening to everyone's questions and remembering where certain cards are is key to being able to work out how to complete your sets – the winner is the first to finish their cards.

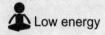 Low energy

Devilishly Difficult Diplomat

The set-up and aim of this variant are the same as standard Diplomat, but the way of getting there is a bit more tricky and better suited to older players. In your turn, rather than requesting cards you can ask as many yes-no questions to other players as you like ('Do you have any even-numbered clubs?', 'Do you have any sevens?') until you get a no. Alternatively, you can request specific cards are 'laid out', in order to form sets of four with the cards in your hand. Remembering what everyone has asked and answered over the course of a few turns, and using a bit of deduction, you eventually get to the point where you can finish a set by making requests like 'Mollie, lay out the three of diamonds. Noah, lay out the three of spades. Matty, lay out the three of clubs. I have the three of hearts.'

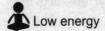 Low energy

Cheat

Also known by a significantly ruder name

Age: 8 and up

Players: 3 and up

What you need: A deck of cards

How to play: If playing with more than five people, try shuffling two decks of cards together. Deal out all cards. The player to the dealer's left starts by placing, face down, any amount of cards and saying – whether truthfully or not – what they're putting down. The hand needs to all be of the same value, i.e. two tens or three threes. The next player continues by playing cards one rank higher, in whatever quantity they can (or feel confident lying about). Whenever you suspect someone of cheating, shouting 'Cheat!' as they play their hand means they have to reveal the cards played. If they were cheating (and players can lie not just about the value of the cards they're placing down, but the quantity), they take the whole pile. If they were telling the truth, you take it. The winner is the first player to get rid of all of their cards.

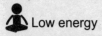 Low energy

501 *Getting rid of all your cards is also the aim of Irish Snap [56].*

Cheerful Cheat

In this variation, shuffle two or three decks together to play (it helps to have big hands). Players don't have to increase the rank of the cards they play, but they do have to match the quantity – two eights has to be followed by two of something else, for instance.

 Low energy

Light Rummy

There are umpteen complicated rummy variations out there, but this provides a nice starting point

Age: 9 and up

Players: 2 to 4

What you need: A deck of cards

How to play: The aim is to get three of something and four of something else – either all of the same rank or a run of cards of the same suit in a row. A winning hand could be, for instance, three sixes and the nine, ten, jack and queen of hearts (or four sixes and the nine, ten and jack of hearts). Deal seven cards to each player, and turn over the top card of the remaining pile to begin the discard pile. Players have to pick a card up, either from the face-down pile of remaining cards or the discard pile, and discard one. Keep an eye on what your opponents are discarding to make sure you aren't trying to collect the same thing, and be ready to rethink your whole plan based on picking one key card up.

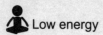 Low energy

Big-hand Rummy

In this variation of rummy, if picking a card up from the discard pile, you also have to pick up everything beneath it. Because this means having more than seven cards, you can place down any combination of three or four cards that go together – either a sequence in order or multiple cards of the same rank – with the aim being to get rid of all of your cards.

 Low energy

Spit

Age: 10 and up

Players: 2

What you need: A deck of cards

How to play: Sit face to face. Each player has a five-card hand and a fifteen-card draw pile. Two cards are placed face down on the table between players, with a pile of five cards (the 'flip pile') next to each one. Counting 'One, two, three, go', both players turn over the cards in the middle. You can place a card from your hand down if it is one above or one below the cards on either side – i.e., if a seven is shown, you can put a six or an eight down, and then keep going until you can't play any more (aces are both above kings and below twos, so you can go queen-king-ace-two-ace-king, for example). As your hand gets smaller, replenish it from your draw pile to keep five cards in your hand. When neither of you can put any more cards down, count down again and simultaneously turn another card over from the flip piles. If the flip piles run out, turn over the piles of played cards and use them. The first player to get rid of all of their cards is the winner.

 Low energy

California Spit

Similar to regular Spit, but with a different set-up. Split the deck into two. Each player deals themselves a Solitaire-like hand, five columns wide: deal one card face up, then four face down to start the five columns, then one face up on the second column and one each face down on the third, fourth and fifth, then one face up on the third and one each face down on the fourth and fifth, the one face up on the fourth and one face down on the fifth, then one face up on the fifth. The remaining cards are the flip pile. As you play your cards, turn over the ones beneath them or reposition them so you always have five cards visible, both to you and to your opponent. When you play all your cards, slap the pile you think is smaller and deal yourself another hand from them. It may take several rounds, but the winner is the first one to get rid of all their cards – when one player is down to just one card, you only have one flip pile, and when they play their card, slapping the pile of zero (i.e., where the other pile used to be) wins the game.

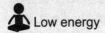 Low energy

Literature

A taxing team game of memory and tactics

Age: 10 and up

Players: 6 or 8

What you need: A deck of cards

How to play: Put the twos aside. Split into two teams, sitting in alternating order around the table. Deal out the 48 remaining cards. The object of the game is to acquire 'half-suits' – either 3 to 8 ('low') or 9 to A ('high') of one suit, and when a player gets one they put it face up on the table for all to see. Player one begins by asking a player on the opposite team for a specific card – it has to be one from a half-suit they already have one or more cards from. If that player has the card requested, they give it to player one. Player one can keep requesting specific cards until they get a no. Everyone is advised to pay attention to what other players have and don't have. If you figure out your team has all of a half-suit distributed between them, on your turn you can declare it – 'Low hearts, I have the 3 and 4, Isla has the 5, 6 and 8 and Ted has the 7'. If you're right, you win the half-suit. If you're wrong, the other team wins it. The team that gets the most half-suits wins the game.

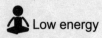 Low energy

Knacker Your Neighbour

A fast-paced game, played in the Himalayas, that works well with a big group sitting around a table

Age: 10 and up

Players: 4 to 20

What you need: A deck of cards and pennies or counters for lives

How to play: Everyone starts with three lives. The dealer deals one card to everyone, face down. Going clockwise around the table, starting with the player to the left of the dealer, everyone has to decide whether to keep their card or swap it with the player to their left, without seeing what they have. When it gets back to the dealer (who either keeps their card or swaps it for one off the top of the remaining deck), everyone reveals their card, and the player with the lowest one (with aces low) loses a life. The winner is the last player left alive.

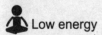 Low energy

Bad Neighbours

The same rules as Knacker Your Neighbour with two small changes. Firstly, if you have a king – the highest card – and a player wants to swap with you, you can refuse by turning your king over and revealing it to the whole table. Secondly, you go around twice, potentially allowing you to redeem earlier mistakes, potentially doubling down on them.

 Low energy

Pencil-and-Paper Games

Tic-Tac-Toe

A game so simple it probably doesn't need to be here, but one that can be expanded and riffed on

Age: 5 and up

Players: 2

What you need: Paper and pencil

How to play: A quick, simple game of lines and loops. Two horizontal lines are drawn and criss-crossed with two vertical ones, making an open nine-square grid. One player is assigned O, one player X and, by taking it in turns to place their symbol in a square, both try to form a line of three, either vertically, horizontally or diagonally.

 Low energy

Tic-Tac-Toenail

Like regular tic-tac-toe, but instead of one player being X and one being O, both players can play either symbol, and the winner is the first person to complete a matching row of three.

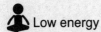 Low energy

Nine Holes

This game was played by the builders of Westminster Abbey – there are grids embedded in the cloisters

Age: 5 and up

Players: 2

What you need: Six coins – three of one colour and three of another – plus paper and pen

How to play: Like tic-tac-toe, the object of Nine Holes is to try and get three in a row, but unlike that game, diagonals don't count, and your pieces move. Draw a tic-tac-toe grid, and each take it in turns to place a coin down. When all coins have been placed, turns then involve moving any of your coins to any unoccupied space. This also works as a beach game, played in the sand with different coloured pebbles or shells.

 Low energy

Sliding Holes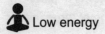

Like Nine Holes, but rather than moving your pieces to any unoccupied spot, you can only move to an adjacent spot. However, diagonal lines of three are acceptable.

 Low energy

Battleship

Age: 6 and up

Players: 2

What you need: Paper and pens, something to put between you to block each other's view

How to play: Each player draws two grids, ten squares by ten squares, labelling the rows 1–10 and the columns A–J. In one grid, they then draw several 'boats' by colouring in squares – an aircraft carrier (five squares long), a battleship (four squares long), a submarine (three), a destroyer (three) and a patrol boat (two), vertically or horizontally. Players then take it in turns launching missiles at each other by calling out a co-ordinate, keeping track of where they fire on their other grid (and where they are fired upon). When fired upon, a player reports a miss or a hit (specifying the type of craft hit if so, and pointing out when a whole craft is sunk). Take it in turns ('E-3!' 'Miss! F2!' 'Hit, patrol boat! H7!') until one person's fleet is entirely destroyed.

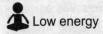 Low energy

> **501** *If you enjoyed the nautical elements of this one, why not take to the seven seas with Ships-and-Lifeboats (367)?*

Baddleship

Two key changes can make Battleship more difficult. First, not mentioning what kind of craft has been hit (or confirming when a whole boat has been sunk). Second, and most infuriatingly, removing the regular shape of the ships. So, an aircraft carrier is still five squares, but it doesn't have to be five in a row – it could be an L-shape, or three on one row and two on the next. This way of playing is extremely difficult, and recommended only for older players who find regular Battleship a breeze.

 Low energy

Salvo

This Battleship variation dates from the 1930s and makes for an *extraordinarily* difficult game. Instead of launching one missile at a time, players fire as many missiles as they have boats still afloat. And, instead of hearing where each landed, they get a field report that just gives the quantity of hits and misses. It requires sometimes bombing the same spot twice to be entirely sure if there's anything there or not.

 Low energy

Hangman

The needlessly execution-themed word-guessing classic

Age: 6 and up

Players: 2

What you need: Pencil and paper

How to play: Player one thinks of a word and writes down a dash for each letter. Depending on how difficult you want it to be, they might give a clue – perhaps it's the name of a country, or a food, or somebody both players know. As player two guesses letters, they are placed on the relevant dash if they are in the word, or a line is added to the gallows. If the word is guessed before the hanged man is complete (stand, vertical bar, horizontal bar, diagonal strut, rope, head, body, leg, leg, arm, arm, face), player one wins.

 Low energy

Hang Out, Man

Why does hangman have to be so violent? Swap the gallows for a nice sofa, and beat your opponent not through hanging but through ending up with a drawing of a person simply chilling on a simply drawn couch.

 Low energy

Exquisite Corpse

A gruesome name for a silly way of creating a masterpiece

Age: 6 and up (and feel free to use the less exciting, but also less vampiric, name 'picture consequences' for younger players)

Players: 2 to 4

What you need: Paper and pencils

How to play: Fold the paper twice widthways like a concertina, so it is divided into four equal strips, only one of which is visible. Hidden from the other players, the first player has 2 minutes to draw a head on the top strip – any type of head at all. A penguin's head, an explorer's head, a hammerhead shark, anything, making sure a few lines go just over the fold. They then fold it so only the second strip is visible (complete with those few lines that came over) and give it to the second player, who draws a body. The third does some legs, the fourth some feet. When it's all over, unfolding the page should result in a delightful monstrosity.

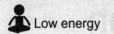 Low energy

Tree of Delights

Draw two lines down the middle of a piece of paper, to represent a tree trunk, then fold it widthways into four and hand it around. Everyone takes it in turns to add to the tree – from sensible things like branches, koalas and birds to more off-piste ones like burglars, trapped kites, underpants being hung up to dry and portals to another realm.

 Low energy

Tin Ha Tai Ping

The title of this game translates from Chinese as 'peace in the world', yet it's fairly, uh, fighty?

Age: 7 and up

Players: 2

What you need: Pencil and paper

How to play: Each player draws a 2x2 grid, then a battle begins. A battle . . . of Rock Paper Scissors (see page 214). Each player's grid is their castle, which they must build up, but a player only gets to build it up one stage at a time by winning a round of Rock Paper Scissors. Only when your castle is fully built up can you use it to attack your opponent. First initial each square in the grid, then add a cannon to each square, then add a fortifying wall to each square. When you have all your cannons and walls in place (i.e., after winning 12 rounds of Rock Paper Scissors), every time you win a round you can attack your opponent, taking away first their fortifying walls, then their cannons, then their initials. Every victory can be used to rebuild your castle or attack your opponent's – pencil is advised for this as it can get extremely messy building and destroying things endlessly. And, of course, you can't attack anyone if you have no cannons. Depending on both luck and tactics, games can last anything from a few minutes to weeks on end.

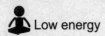 Low energy

Extended Tin Ha Tai Ping

If 'weeks on end' isn't enough for you, you can also play with a 3x3 grid. The centre square doesn't need cannons or fortification, but every other one does.

 Low energy

Consequences

A patchwork approach to creating a surreal narrative

Age: 7 and up

Players: 2 and up

What you need: Paper and pens

How to play: One player writes a very short story, leaving out some important words – a verb here, a noun there, an adjective or two. For instance: 'My name's [*proper noun*],' said the [*adjective*] woman, as she started to [*verb*] past a [*adjective*] [*noun*]. 'I'm here to [*verb*] a [*noun*]'. Without showing anyone the story, they ask for suggestions from the other players ('Ellie, can I have a verb?', 'Vicky, I need an adjective' and so on), and piece together a potentially ridiculous tale. Expect at least a few suggestions of 'smelly', 'toilet' and the like. Then wait for Hollywood to come calling!

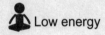 Low energy

SOS

Age: 8 and up

Players: 2

What you need: Paper and pencil

How to play: Like tic-tac-toe, but with a few key differences. First, the board can be as big as you want. Second, instead of playing Xs and Os, you play either S or O, whichever you want to play on each turn, scoring points by completing sequences that say SOS. If you complete an SOS, you get another turn. Keep track of how many each of you get – the player with the most points when the grid is full wins.

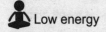 Low energy

...ockey

...erity of a type rarely required

What y... ...per, tape, pencils – long ones with rubbers on the end work best

How to play: Take your sheet of paper and draw even-sized goals at both ends, and as straightforward or complicated a path as you like between them. You can just do a straight broad road from one goal to the other, or a wiggly, windy route. Now tape it down to the table. Then, take it in turns to try to get from your goal to your opponent's goal by placing one finger on top of the pencil's rubber and pushing it along as far as you can before it falls or you go out of bounds. Begin your next turn with the pencil on the end of your last line. First to get to the other player's goal wins.

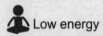 Low energy

501 *Another paper version of a sport: Paper Rugby [29].*

Hockey Smile

The same set-up as normal Pencil Hockey, but players grip their pencils in their teeth. A turn ends when the lead leaves the paper or the course.

 Low energy

Dots

An initially Zen-like experience that turns into a land grab

Age: 8 and up

Players: 2

What you need: Pencil and paper

How to play: Draw a 12x12 grid of dots – 12 rows of 12, about a centimetre apart. If available, each of you should use a different coloured pen. Take it in turns to draw horizontal or vertical lines joining two adjacent dots. The object of the game is to complete as many 1x1 squares as possible, each of which you then colour in (or initial) before taking another turn. When the grid is completely filled, total up how many squares each player has – the one with the most wins.

 Low energy

Different Dots

Experiment with different-sized grids – tactics are very different between playing a brutally quick game on a 3x3 grid and an initially sleepy-paced 20x20.

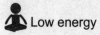 Low energy

Five by Five

Age: 8 and up

Players: 2

What you need: Pencil and paper

How to play: Each player thinks of a five-letter word, and tells the other player the first letter of it. You then try to work out what the other player's word is, writing each guess down and giving them the paper. They draw a circle around any letter in the right place, and underline any correct letters that are in the wrong place. For instance, if the word is CARDS, they're told it's C----. If they guess CHATS, the C and S are circled and the A and R are underlined. Try to get each other's words in five goes or less.

 Low energy

Organisation vs Anarchy

Two of the world's most powerful forces compete on paper

Age: 8 and up

Players: 2

What you need: Pencil and paper

How to play: One player represents Organisation, the other Anarchy. On a 6x6 grid, take it in turns to put either an X or an O in a square – both players can play either one.
Organisation wants to form a line of five of the same symbol (either one), while Anarchy wants to prevent that happening and end up with a full board in which there are no lines of five.

 Low energy

Nine Men's Morris

Looks complicated, starts off simple, gets really complicated again

Age: 8 and up

Players: 2

What you need: Pen and (ideally squared) paper, nine coins or counters of one colour and nine of another

How to play: Draw a big square, 6 squares wide and 6 tall. Now draw a smaller 4x4 one within it, and a 2x2 one within that. Now connect the middle of each line on the smallest square with the middle of each line of the largest one (going through the 4x4 one) and mark each of the 24 corners or intersections with big dots – this is your board. Take it in turns to place one of your coins down on a dot. Any time you manage to form three in a row, this is called a 'mill' and lets you take one of your opponent's pieces off the board (although if some of their pieces are in complete mills and others aren't, you can't opt to remove one from a mill). When all the pieces have been put down, they move by sliding to an adjacent dot. Going back and forth to break and re-form a mill in order to take more and more of your opponent's pieces is absolutely allowed. When one player is down to three pieces, they can move wherever they wish, not just to adjacent spots. However, as soon as a player is down to two pieces, they lose.

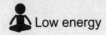 Low energy

Ten Men's Morris

Start with ten pieces each, with the added twist that you can start moving pieces before they've all been placed down, making it all the more complicated and all the more tactical.

 Low energy

Cows and Bulls

Age: 8 and up

Players: 2

What you need: Pencil and paper

How to play: Each player thinks of a four-digit number with no repeated digits and, taking it in turns, tries to guess their opponent's number. After each guess, they're told how many cows (the right digit in the right place) and bulls (the right digit in the wrong place) they have. For instance, if the number is 4583, a guess of 8591 would be one cow (the 5) and one bull (the 8). The first one to successfully figure out the other player's number wins.

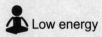 Low energy

Cow-Words and Ver-Bulls

Use four-letter words (without repeated letters) instead of numbers. On the one hand there are 26 different letters, so it feels like it'll be harder, but on the other, there are certain patterns that happen in words, so it all evens out.

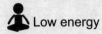 Low energy

Fives Fight

Age: 8 and up

Players: 2

What you need: Pencil and paper

How to play: Each player thinks of a five-letter word without any repeated letters in it. Taking it in turns, one player guesses what the other player's word might be, and is told how many letters their guess shares with the actual word. For instance, if player one's word is TABLE and player two guesses TOWER, that's two, T and E – however, player two is only told 'two', not which ones or their positions or anything else. Going back and forth, by a process of elimination you can work out what letters it can't possibly contain, and eventually guess the other player's word. A good tip is to write the whole alphabet down and cross letters out when they are eliminated – it still might take 20 or so turns to get each other's words, though.

 Low energy

A Bunch of 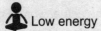 Fives

Up to six people can play at once. In this variation, when a player guesses a word, every other player states how many letters from it are in their secret word. The winner is the first player to be able to name every other player's secret word.

 Low energy

Three Fifteen

A very quick but often incredibly frustrating game involving maths and tactics: mathetactics

Age: 8 and up

Players: 3

What you need: Nothing, although it can't hurt to involve a pen and paper

How to play: The aim of the game is to total exactly 15. Take it in turns selecting numbers from one to nine – each number can only be used once between you. You need to think about what your opponents are doing just as much as your own numbers. Most rounds end in a stalemate, so play until one person has won five times.

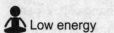 Low energy

Ultimate Tic-Tac-Toe

An infuriating, computer-defying, giant variation

Age: 9 and up

Players: 2

What you need: Pencil and paper

How to play: Draw a really big tic tac-toe-board (the 'global' board), then draw a smaller one within each of its squares (the 'local' boards). One player is X and one is O. X starts by going wherever they want on any local board, but O then has to play in the local board within the square of the global board corresponding with where X has played – i.e., if X plays the top-right corner of the top-left local board, O has to play in the local board at the top-right of the global board, and so on. It sounds confusing at first, but you'll get the hang of it. When each local board is won, a large X or O is drawn across it, and the winner is whoever wins the global board. Warning: this is entirely maddening.

 Low energy

Treble Cross

Squared paper is ideal for this – you play across one row, as wide as you like. Twenty squares wide, 30 squares wide, however wide you wish, but only one square high. Take it in turns to draw an X in one square, and the winner is the player who manages to complete a row of three.

 Low energy

Notakto

An eccentric mathematician's strange, infuriating variation on a classic

Age: 10 and up

Players: 2

What you need: Pencil and paper

How to play: Notakto looks essentially like three games of tic-tac-toe played at once, where both players are X and nobody wants to form a line. Start by drawing three boards, then taking it in turns to place an X in any square. When a row of three is created, that board is dead. The player who completes the row of three on the final board loses the game of Notakto.

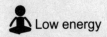 Low energy

Kropki

A Polish strategy game that is up there with the most challenging games in the world

Age: 10 and up

Players: 2

What you need: Squared paper, different-coloured pens

How to play: Decide on the boundaries of your game – a full page of squared paper will generally do it. Take it in turns drawing dots where the lines on the paper cross. The aim of the game is to create shapes that entirely enclose some of your opponent's dots when joined by vertical, horizontal or diagonal lines – when you put down a dot that finishes such a shape, you draw the line connecting them all and win 1 point for each of your opponent's trapped dots. You end up with something that looks a bit like a map drawn by someone who has only ever had maps described to them and never actually seen one. This can easily end up being incredibly time-consuming, extraordinarily frustrating and occasionally relationship-destroying.

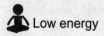 Low energy

Sprouts

Somewhere between deadly simple and extraordinarily complicated, this game takes a bit of explaining but is easy to pick up

Age: 10 and up

Players: 2

What you need: Pen and paper

How to play: Sprouts involves joining dots up with curved lines. Players start by putting one dot down each. Then, player one joins the two dots with a curved line, adding another dot somewhere along it. Player two draws a curved line either between two dots or from one dot in a loop back to itself, and adds another dot somewhere along that line, and so on – every turn involves a curved line and a new dot. However, the curved lines can't cross one another, and no dot can have more than three lines coming out of it (particularly limiting if planning to return to the same dot). You can end up with something weirdly beautiful, that looks like it should be carved into the desert floor for aliens to read. You can also end up with a big confusing mess. The last player able to make a move wins.

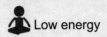 Low energy

Galactic Spacebucks

Ever so strategic and incredibly frustrating

Age: 10 and up

Players: 2

What you need: Pencil and paper, one coin or counter

How to play: Both players start with 50 galactic spacebucks. Draw a 'board' of seven squares in a row, with the counter in the middle one and a planet drawn in the outermost squares. On each turn, players write down an amount of spacebucks then reveal them to one another, moving the counter one square towards the home planet of whoever pays the most galactic spacebucks. However, they don't get those spacebucks back – with each turn, each player's spacebucks account dwindles, so they really need to make those 50 spacebucks work for them. Play until the counter lands on someone's home planet – they are the galactic spacewinner.

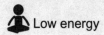 Low energy

Rare Danger

An anagram of 'rearranged', involving muddling and re-muddling words

Age: 10 and up

Players: 4 or more

What you need: Pens and paper, a timer

How to play: Everyone is presented with a long word – nine-plus letters – and has 1 minute to write down as many words of three or more letters as they can using the letters from it. Holding the word up when announcing it is definitely helpful, as nothing is more infuriating than coming up with perfect anagrams of the wrong word. After the minute, go through everyone's words – players score the amount of points as there are letters in each of their words, with a bonus point for every word of over six letters.

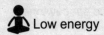 Low energy

Aquamarine Gun*

*Unique Anagram

Players try to come up with the longest unique word they can using the available letters – they score no points if someone else comes up with the same one. This requires thinking tactically about what your opponents are likely to come up with – an offbeat five-letter word might be a better bet than an obvious eight, but are you the only person thinking that?

 Low energy

Outdoor Games

Find Some Fun: In The Playground

Use this high-tech, futuristic method to find a game to play, because why should you have to do all the work yourself?

Hey guys, are you in the mood to be really, really quiet?

No

Yes

Anyone fancy doing a bit of prep before the game starts?

Silent Ball [359] is the game for you. Ssssshhhhhh . . .

Yes

No

I Am Not a Number [277] needs a bit of work doing beforehand but can keep lots of people busy for ages.

Got a ball?

Yes

Are there things to hide behind, and is the landscape generally conducive to stealth and hiding?

Cops and Robbers [274] or Capture the Flag [275] should do you perfectly.

No

Yes

You could do a lot worse than Duck Duck Goose [345], you know . . .

Okay, are we talking spreading out over a big wide area?

No

If you want a ball, you can probably find a ball. Do you want a ball?

No

No

Yes

Yes

Try Qiu [264], or if you have a bat as well, Non-Stop Cricket [265].

Ball Games

Piggy in the Middle

A friendly game of catch, with the friendliness replaced by DECEIT and INTERCEPTION

Age: 6 and up

Players: 3

What you need: A ball

How to play: One player – the piggy – tries to intercept the ball as the other two players throw it back and forth. If they do, then the player who threw it swaps with them and becomes the piggy. Jumping, sneaking off to one side while the piggy's back is turned and experimenting with throwing the ball really high are all encouraged.

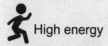 High energy

501 *For another game involving hogs, try Pig [44].*

Pork and Mash

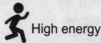

All the usual rules of piggy in the middle, but with one added, intense element: the hot-potato rule, where the ball has to be thrown immediately. If anyone holds on to the ball for more than a second, they become the piggy.

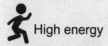 High energy

Eliminate

In which a wall is a key player

Age: 6 and up

Players: 3 and up

What you need: A tennis ball

How to play: Everyone starts with three lives. A player throws the ball against the wall so it then bounces back towards them, at which point another player catches it and does the same. However, if a player catches it before it bounces on the ground, the player who threw the ball has to run and touch the wall as quickly as possible, while the player who caught it throws it at them, trying to tag them in the legs (softly). If they're hit before touching the wall, they lose a life. Last player standing wins.

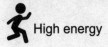 High energy

World Cup

A miniature Mundial

Age: 6 and up

Players: 4 and up

What you need: A football, a goal

How to play: One player goes in goal. The others then compete to score first, in a free-for-all. Once a player has scored, they leave the pitch. When all players but one have scored, start again, but with that player out. Keep going until only two players are left in the World Cup Final, at which point the first to score wins.

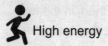 High energy

World Cup of Everything

This tournament format, losing one player per round until there is a champion, works for pretty much any ball sport, plus doesn't always need a goalie. Got a basketball hoop? World Cup of Basketball. Got a tennis ball and a tree? World Cup of Throwing the Tennis Ball at The Tree.

 High energy

Downball

A mysterious handball/tennis/volleyball hybrid originating in the playgrounds of Hong Kong

Age: 7 and up

Players: 2

What you need: A tennis ball and a defined 'court' – a line on the ground and designated 'out of bounds'

How to play: One player serves by throwing the ball up, then slapping it with their hand so it bounces once on their side of the line then crosses it. Their opponent needs to slap it back, so it bounces once before crossing the line. It's allowed to bounce once in your court before being returned. If the ball bounces twice before being returned, bounces twice before crossing the line, goes straight over the line without bouncing, or goes out of bounds without bouncing on your opponent's side then either a point is scored (if serving) or service changes hands. Only the serving player can score, and the first to 11 wins.

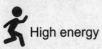 High energy

Doubles Downball

Like regular downball, but with four players – two on each side. One or both players can touch the ball, but not catch it – volleyball-style set-ups where you half-catch the ball but set it up for your partner to slam are particularly effective.

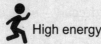

High energy

Post-Apocalypse Golf

Who needs an 18-hole course when you can just put loads of stuff in the way of one hole?

Age: 7 and up

Players: 2 to 4

What you need: You can get by with one ball and one club (or something that approximates them), pen and paper to keep score

How to play: When the zombie uprising comes, golf courses will be no-go areas. Therefore, wannabe golfers are going to have to learn to improvise. You only need one hole (or mark on the ground) – players take it in turns to decide the teeing-off point and place obstacles in the way. Play as imaginative an 18-hole course as you can – things like tunnels, ramps and incredibly annoying obstructions are all relatively easy to create.

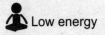 Low energy

Four Square

Four players, one ball, infinite possibilities

Age: 7 and up

Players: 4 and up

What you need: Chalk, a tennis ball

How to play: Use chalk to draw a big square on the ground – 3 metres by 3 metres-ish – and divide it into four equal-sized squares, numbered one to four going clockwise. One person stands in each square. Players start by throwing the ball to one another going clockwise, making it bounce in the square of the person they're throwing it to before it's caught. Go faster and faster and faster until someone makes a mistake (by missing or mis-throwing), at which point they swap places with the person in the square 'below' them. Try to get to number one and hold on to it – if you can successfully stay there for five goes, consider yourself a champion.

 High energy

More Square

Every time anyone misses, the person who threw the ball to them gets to create a rule. Does a certain player have to shout every time they throw? Does the direction of play change every six passes?

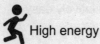 High energy

Horse

Ideally played on a New York basketball court, but just as good played against a tree in Devon

Age: 8 and up

Players: 2

What you need: A football, a basketball or a netball and a hoop (or an improvised one – a mark on a wall, a designated branch of a tree, and so on)

How to play: The aim of the game is *not* to be the first player to receive all of the letters of HORSE. Take it in turns taking a shot at the target. If you make it, your opponent has to match your shot from the exact place you are standing or they get a letter, while if you miss it and your opponent then makes it, you get one.

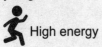 High energy

Donkey

The rules of Horse are universal enough to apply to any sporting equipment, really. Make a mark on the ground and use a golf club and ball, or even a snooker cue and billiard ball – whatever is around. It's a good format!

 High energy

Wally

In most sporting title fights, the title is desirable – not this one!

Age: 8 and up

Players: 2

What you need: A football

How to play: Wally is played, like the name suggests, against a wall. A certain area of wall is designated as the playing area, and players take it in turns kicking the ball against the wall, never allowing it to come to a standstill. If they miss the designated area of wall, or let the ball come to a standstill, they get a letter (like in the game HORSE) of the word 'WALLY'. The first complete Wally loses.

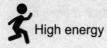 High energy

High, High, Up in the Sky

A game in which tall buildings come in very handy

Age: 8 and up

Players: 2 and up

What you need: A tennis ball, a high wall

How to play: In turn, players throw the ball so it bounces off a wall as high as they can. When it comes down, they jump, so that they are in the air when it bounces. The next player then catches it before it bounces again. Failure to be in the air during the bounce, or to catch it before bounce two, costs you a life. Everyone starts with three lives, and the last player standing wins.

 High energy

Paddling Pool Battleship

Depth charges, big splashes and paper boats you'd better not get too attached to

Age: 8 and up

Players: 2 and up

What you need: A paddling pool, paper, a bouncy ball or squash ball

How to play: Every player makes a paper boat from a sheet of A4, folding it however they wish. The boats are floated in the paddling pool, and players take it in turns to drop (not throw) the ball from 20 cm or so above the pool surface, trying to sink their opponents' boats. Keep playing until only one boat is afloat.

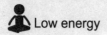 Low energy

Long-Distance Battleship

Throw a dice. Take that many steps away from the pool and, using an underarm throw, try to sink your opponents' boats but not your own.

 Low energy

Headers and Volleys

A beloved balls-in-the-air playground staple

Age: 8 and up

Players: 6 to 10

What you need: A football, a goal

How to play: Form two teams. There are no goalkeepers – everyone can both score and save goals. The team with the ball throw it from one to another, trying to get into a position where they can set a teammate up for a goal (meanwhile, the opponents try to intercept it). They do this by throwing it to them to either be headed or volleyed in – the ball can't be kicked from the ground, and a goal can't be scored from a throw. Score 2 points for a goal and 1 for a shot on target that gets saved. The first team to 10 points wins.

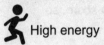 High energy

Runs

Like baseball stripped down to its simplest form: no bat, just bases and a ball

Age: 8 and up

Players: 6 and up

What you need: A ball, plus two things to act as bases – lines on the ground, shoes, hats, anything

How to play: Position the bases about 5 metres apart. Two people are fielders, and everyone else is a runner. One fielder goes on each base, and half the players start behind each one. The runners try to score as many runs as possible – getting from one base to the other without being tagged by the ball while between bases – while the fielders try to tag them out, either by touching the ball to them or throwing it at their legs. Runners have to keep their own score, so honesty is key.

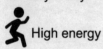 High energy

Jumbo Catch

Try to throw the ball so high it comes down with bits of Moon on it

Age: 6 and up

Players: 3 to 6

What you need: A ball

How to play: One player is the thrower, who launches the ball as high in the air as possible, while the catchers compete to be under it. Catch the ball, get 1 point. Fumble or let it through your hands, lose 1 point. Rotate thrower each time. First to 5 wins.

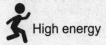 High energy

Jumbo Turbo Catch

Everyone plays to 1,000 points, with the point value of the catch yelled by the thrower while the ball is in the air. They can shout it as early or late in the throw as they wish, and can throw in the occasional negative number to keep catchers on their toes.

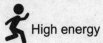 High energy

Super Jumbo Turbo Catch

The thrower can add in extra options, yelled while the ball is in flight: Millionaire (an instant win for the catcher), Broke (straight to zero), Bomb (the catcher's score is halved), Thief (the catcher can steal another catcher's points), Freeze (the catcher has to stay totally still for the next throw) and anything else that takes your fancy.

 High energy

Butts Up

Tennis balls and sore bottoms: a dance as old as time

Age: 10 and up

Players: 4 to 8

What you need: A tennis ball, a wall

How to play: Players throw the ball against the wall and catch it. If anyone misses it, or somehow manages to miss the wall, they have to run and tag the wall before anyone else gets a chance to pick the ball up and throw it against the wall – if they manage the tag, they're fine, but if the ball is thrown against the wall, they have a (pretend) star above their head. When anyone gets to three stars, they stand facing the wall and everyone gets one chance to throw the ball (softly) at their rear end.

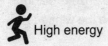 High energy

Other Equipment

Hosepipe Limbo

How low can you go? And how wet can you get?

Age: 5 and up

Players: 2 and up

What you need: A hosepipe

How to play: Squirt a jet of water out of the hose, starting at child's head height (this game works very well in concert with filling a paddling pool), and have them limbo under it. Then bring it down by 10cm or so, and repeat, and keep going, again and again, lower and lower. The winner is whoever manages to stay dry longest, and their grand prize is being completely soaked. It's not always great to be the winner.

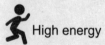 High energy

> **501** *Combine limbo skills and jumping with Higher and Higher [141].*

Hopscotch

A playground classic, easily made with chalk or tape

Age: 6 and up

Players: 1 and up

What you need: Chalk or tape and a small stone

How to play: Mark out a hopscotch court on the ground – ten squares of 30x30cm, alternating between single ones and two adjoining ones, numbered one to ten. A player starts by hopping and jumping the full course, there and back – hopping on one foot in single squares and using two feet for side-by-side squares, one in each square. Then, the player throws a stone into square one, and does the course again, skipping that square both on the way out and the way back. Then they throw the stone into square two, and so on. If playing with multiple players, standing on a line or a square with the stone in it means stopping your turn and letting the next player have theirs, picking up where you left off when you rejoin.

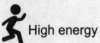 High energy

Hectic Hopscotch

While you've got the chalk out, why not add extra bits to each square – perhaps people have to blow a raspberry when their foot touches number seven, or spin around while hopping on number nine. Use your imagination and see how difficult, silly or both you can make it.

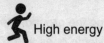 High energy

Hose Showdown

The Wild West meets Gardeners' World

Age: 6 and up

Players: 2 and up

What you need: A hosepipe with a trigger attachment, household odds and ends to make targets with

How to play: Make as many targets as possible, potentially in multiple stages (for instance, a plastic cup balanced on a plastic bottle balanced on an upright shoebox, where the cup has to be dealt with before the bottle, and so on) and distribute them around the garden. Players can either take it in turns to do two-second bursts of hose fire (strictly enforced by those around them), or use a simple dice or coin game to earn seconds of pressurised water spray. Experiment with point values, squirt duration and just how big a mess you can make with something theoretically designed for cleaning.

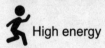 High energy

Hose Bowling

Use (non-glass) bottles or cans to set up an outdoor bowling alley, then play according to proper bowling rules (see page 15), using the briefest of trigger-squeezes for each bowl. Holding the trigger down for too long incurs a five-pin penalty.

 High energy

Higher and Higher

A game based around a really key decision: when do you switch from one mode to the next?

Age: 6 and up

Players: 3 and up

What you need: A skipping rope or length of string

How to play: Two players hold the rope horizontally at ankle level, and the others jump over it. Then they hold it slightly higher – knee level – and everyone jumps over it again. The rope keeps getting higher, and players reach a point where they have to choose whether to try to jump really high or limbo really low. Players are out when they don't make it, and the last player standing wins.

 High energy

501 *A fan of the jumping element? The Floor is Lava [11] involves barely touching the ground at all.*

Pitching Pennies

An age-old game of chucking coins

Age: 6 and up

Players: 2 to 6

What you need: Five pennies each, potentially some chalk

How to play: Play against a high wall, marking out an area if necessary, about as wide and long as a parking space. Everyone then takes it in turns to throw a penny at the wall, and whoever ends up closest to it wins all the pennies. When someone is out of pennies, they are out of the game.

 Low energy

Piles of Cash

Coins have to hit the wall before landing – if they hit the ground first, they don't count. Plus, if one coin lands partially on top of another, it counts as nearer the wall even if it's further away.

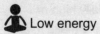 Low energy

Horseshoes?
Yourshoes!

The game horseshoes has been played for centuries, but unless you come from a family of blacksmiths, you might not have many knocking about . . .

Age: 8 and up

Players: 2 and up

What you need: A pair of shoes each with the laces tied together, a fence post or cricket stump, paper to keep score

How to play: Take it in turns throwing your shoes at the post. Score 3 points for a 'ringer' (where a line drawn between the toes of the shoes would be on the other side of the post to the laces), 2 points for a 'toucher' (where one shoe is touching the post) and 1 point for a 'knocker' (where a shoe touches the post but keeps moving and lands away from it). Score 5 for a 'wrapper', where the shoes wrap themselves around the post. First to 25 points wins.

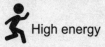High energy

Fighting Chickens

A bit of ground-based roughhousing

Age: 8 and up

Players: 4 and up

What you need: Nothing

How to play: Everyone squats on one leg, which is harder than it sounds – do a regular squat then lift one leg and put it on the opposite knee. Players then barge and jostle each other by hopping, wriggling around and launching themselves into one another. The last player to have to lower their other foot (or, you know, fall over) wins.

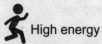 High energy

501 *Which came first, the chicken or the egg? No idea, but give an Egg and Spoon Race [321] a go and see who comes first in that.*

Frisbee Golf

If no frisbee is to hand, use anything you can throw and adjust distances accordingly. Anvil golf? Short holes

Age: 10 and up

Players: 2 to 4

What you need: A frisbee each – ideally as similar in dimensions as possible but all visually distinct

How to play: In a large park, take it in turns choosing a 'hole' – an object or area reasonably far away that you can hit with a frisbee and not lose it. Players try to get there and hit it with their frisbees in as few throws as possible, picking them up from where they land for their next shot. Play 18 holes, using a par-three scoring system (i.e., if you hit the object after three throws, score 0; if you do it in two, score -1; if you do it in six, score 3; lowest score wins).

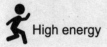 High energy

Travel
Games

Find Some Fun: On The Road

Use this high-tech, futuristic method to find a game to play, because why should you have to do all the work yourself?

Are you on a really long car journey?

Yes

No

Is there a lot to see out of the window?

Take advantage of all that space by playing Tag [259].

No

Yes

The Alphabet Game [168] or The Minister's Cat [165] can keep you going for ages.

Are you on the motorway?

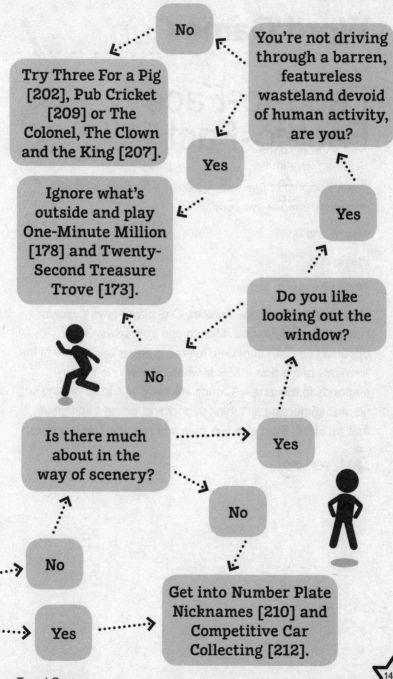

No

You're not driving through a barren, featureless wasteland devoid of human activity, are you?

Try Three For a Pig [202], Pub Cricket [209] or The Colonel, The Clown and the King [207].

Yes

Yes

Ignore what's outside and play One-Minute Million [178] and Twenty-Second Treasure Trove [173].

Do you like looking out the window?

No

Yes

Is there much about in the way of scenery?

No

Yes

No

Get into Number Plate Nicknames [210] and Competitive Car Collecting [212].

Word Games

Face-to-Face
Fact-to-Fact

Quick scraping of one's knowledge banks combined with potentially intense eye contact

Age: 5 and up

Players: 2

What you need: Nothing

How to play: Face one another. One player says a factual sentence – for instance: 'Milk comes from cows.' Their opponent says another one, related in some way to one of the elements of the first – 'Milk is white.' Player one then responds to that one – 'Clouds are white' – and so on and so on until someone can't think of anything, or says something that isn't true. Start with five lives and see who lasts longest.

 Low energy

Wordhammer

Word association, beloved of both psychiatrists and mallet-wielding entertainers

Age: 5 and up

Players: 2 plus an optional master of ceremonies

What you need: Nothing

How to play: Start with a word, any word, and go back and forth from person to person, each offering up a word connected to the last in some way (i.e., if one person says 'car', the other could respond 'wheel', 'driver', 'vehicle', 'journey' and so on). The word has to be connected to the one *immediately* before it, though – you're not making a list on one subject, you're specifically responding to one word. If you repeat a word, take too long to think of one, or come up with something not associated with the previous word, the other player gets 1 point (this is where the optional scorekeeper/master of ceremonies comes in). First to 5 wins.

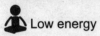 Low energy

Word Dissociation

Like the game above, but the exact opposite – try to come up with a word completely disconnected from the one before it. It's harder than it sounds – our brains automatically try to find patterns and connections. If you can successfully argue that your opponent's word is in fact connected with yours, you win 1 point. First to 5 wins.

 Low energy

One-Sentence Saga

Age: 5 and up

Players: 2 and up

What you need: Nothing

How to play: Create a story, one sentence at a time. Simple as that. Player one starts a tale, player two continues it, and so on. There's no real winner (other than the world of literature), but players can be asked for a new sentence if their suggestion doesn't logically follow on from the previous one. 'Will this game inevitably turn lavatorial?' you ask. Yes. Scholars have found 90 per cent of One-Sentence Saga games involve variations of 'Then he/she/they did a poo' within a minute and a half [citation needed].

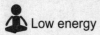 Low energy

One-Word Odyssey

Do your very best to create a comprehensible story, taking it in turns to contribute one word at a time. Beginning with 'Once' 'upon' 'a' 'time' 'there' 'was' 'a' is a nice way to get the rhythm going, and then just see where you end up.

 Low energy

Once Upon a Time

Tell a story using four words at once. The first person needs to start with 'Once upon a time', but after that you're free to go wherever you like. Four words is often enough to set people challenges – snippets that run out, like 'There was a massive . . .' or 'Then they heard a . . .' force the next player to think on their feet.

 Low energy

Say What You See

Each player does a sentence at a time, but something viewable outside the window must be included in each one. The story you end up with might not exactly be Dickens-level ('Once upon a time there was a seagull.' 'One day the seagull went to a coffee shop.' 'In the coffee shop there was a bin.' 'The bin had a picture of a cloud on it.'), but that guy hasn't written anything good for ages anyway.

 Low energy

I Packed My Bag

Fictional shopping that swiftly gets surreal

Age: 5 and up

Players: 2 and up

What you need: Nothing

How to play: 'I packed my bag, and in it I took . . .' begins player one, putting anything they like in their bag. Let's say they go for a sausage. Player two adds something to the list: 'I packed my bag, and in it I took a sausage and a pot noodle.' Player three adds something else: 'I packed my bag, and in it I took a sausage, a pot noodle and a trombone.' Everyone keeps adding something to the list, going as silly as they like, until it becomes impossible to remember and everything descends into chaos.

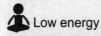 Low energy

> **501** *What people choose to pack can give you an insight into how their minds work. Put that to the test in Ask the Brain [163].*

A Bag Contains Doodahs

An alternative way of playing involves adding items in alphabetical order – something beginning with A followed by something beginning with B and so on. While this makes it easier to work out what comes next, rounds are also likely to end up lasting longer, resulting in everyone having to reel off incredibly lengthy lists.

 Low energy

21

Quick, devious and laden with traps

Age: 6 and up

Players: 2

What you need: Nothing

How to play: Take it in turns to say either one or two consecutive numbers – you're trying to trap the other player into saying '21'. So, player one starts with either 'one' or 'one, two' and so on. Whoever ends up saying 21 loses. Play until one player has won five times.

 Low energy

21 And Over

Every round, the winner gets to add a new rule – blowing a raspberry for odd numbers, saying 'plop' instead of multiples of five, closing your eyes while speaking, anything. By round six, nothing will make sense.

 Low energy

Yes No Black White

Can you have a sensible conversation while avoiding very common words?

Age: 6 and up

Players: 2 and up

What you need: Nothing

How to play: One player is the interrogator and must ask everyone else questions, attempting to get them to say any of the 'forbidden words' – yes, no, black and white. The other players must answer the questions without saying any of the words by being as linguistically creative as possible.

 Low energy

The Russian Ambassador's Ball

In a popular Russian variation, one person is invited to a fancy ball, and the others grill them on what their plans are – what they will wear, how they will dance and so on – without them saying yes, no, black or white or laughing.

 Low energy

Top-Secret Password

Age: 6 and up

Players: 4

What you need: Nothing

How to play: Split into two teams of two. Each team thinks of a secret password – generally an object. One player whispers it to a member of the opposing team (or hands it over on a piece of paper), who has to communicate it to their teammate in ten or fewer single-word clues. After each clue, two guesses are allowed, to be responded to only with 'yes' or 'no'. Score 1 point for every question needed, and after five goes through each, the team with the lowest score wins.

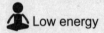 Low energy

Top-Secret Rule

One team thinks of a secret rule, which they then have to follow when answering questions put to them by the other team. For instance, answering all questions with other questions, integrating animals into every answer or answering in a high-pitched Scottish accent. The other team can ask up to five questions of any sort before guessing what the rule is.

 Low energy

Sixty Winks

A refreshingly quiet game that you absolutely can't play while driving.

Age: 6 and up

Players: Any number

What you need: A timer, paper and pencil to keep score

How to play: One person is designated timekeeper. After they count down from five, all the players close their eyes for what they consider to be 1 minute. They can't open their eyes or speak at all, and when they think exactly a minute has passed, they open their eyes and signal to the timekeeper. Score 1 point for every second off 60 you are, whether too long or too short, and after five rounds, lowest scorer wins. Giggling or talking counts as opening your eyes.

 Low energy

Hammersmith or Bust

The same rules as sixty winks, except the timekeeper picks a different length of time every round, and going over by even one second gets you 30 points.

 Low energy

Fortunately/ Unfortunately

A collectively improvised story of myriad ups and downs

Age: 8 and up

Players: 2 or more

What you need: Nothing

How to play: One player starts off a story, with 'Today I went to . . .' Subsequent players continue it, alternating between starting sentences with 'Fortunately . . .' and 'Unfortunately . . .'. For instance, 'Today I went to the hospital.' 'Fortunately, they concluded I was fine.' 'Unfortunately, while telling me that, they robbed me.' 'Fortunately, the hospital was equipped with CCTV.' 'Unfortunately there was a power cut.' 'Fortunately . . .' and so on. There's no winner or loser, you just end up with a deeply strange emotional rollercoaster of a tale.

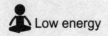 Low energy

Animal Psychiatrist

Sigmund Freud meets Sir David Attenborough

Age: 8 and up

Players: 2

What you need: Nothing

How to play: One person is the psychiatrist, while the other secretly decides on an animal to 'be'. The psychiatrist then presents them with hypothetical situations to try and diagnose what animal they are. 'A ball rolls up to you. What do you do with it?' 'A farmer pats you on the head. What happens?' 'It's dinner time. What are you going to have?' After five such scenarios, the psychiatrist has to diagnose what kind of animal they're dealing with.

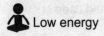 Low energy

Meet in the Middle

Can you end up completely in sync?

Age: 8 and up

Players: 2

What you need: Nothing

How to play: Both players count down from three and then say a word – any word at all – at the same time. The aim is to end up saying the same word as one another, so they then count down again and say a new word somewhere between their previous ones, and so on. For instance, if one of them said 'hammer' and one of them said 'chicken', for their second word one might go for 'armadillo' because it's something hard that is also an animal, while the other might opt for 'tenderiser' because it's a bit like a hammer and used on meat. Keep going until you get there.

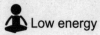 Low energy

Ask the Brain

A game where the actual facts don't matter

Age: 8 and up

Players: 2

What you need: Pen and paper

How to play: One person is designated The Brain. Players take it in turns to ask The Brain a specific question with a numerical answer (say, the height of the tallest mountain in the world in metres, or the age of the youngest president ever), and The Brain writes down what they think the answer is. The other players then say what they think The Brain has written down – not the *actual* answer, the answer they think The Brain has gone for. Closest wins.

 Low energy

501 *Another game of inaccurate statements: Cheat [78].*

Sorry I'm Late

A game of ever-so-familiar excuses

Age: 8 and up

Players: 2 and up

What you need: Nothing

How to play: Players take it in turns to apologise to everyone else for their tardiness. The thing is, their excuse is the plot of a film or book everyone is familiar with, although they can't use any of the words from the title. Anything from 'Sorry I'm late, I rubbed a lamp and a genie came out' to 'Sorry I'm late, there were these spotted dogs – loads of them, probably over 99 . . .' Keep going until the others work it out.

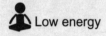 Low energy

The Minister's Cat

How descriptive can you be about a fictional feline?

Age: 8 and up

Players: 2 and up

What you need: Nothing

How to play: One player begins talking about a fictional cat owned by a fictional minister, using an adjective beginning with A, such as 'The minister's cat is an atrocious cat.' Everyone else in turn must do the same, using a different adjective beginning with A, until it is the first player's turn again – they do one final adjective beginning with A, then the second player starts a round of Bs, and so on. If anyone can't think of a word, well, that's a shame.

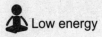 Low energy

A Bureaucrat's Cat, Described Elegantly: Fairly Good, Huh

Instead of everyone contributing an adjective starting with the same letter, one adjective per letter is used, but with all the adjectives preceding it retained – the fourth player might talk about how the minister's cat was an abominable, beastly, cute, deadly cat, for instance.

 Low energy

Ministry of Everything

There's a limit to how long anyone can talk about one made-up moggy. Describe whatever you want. 'The graphics in my new video game are . . .', 'Your school report describes you as . . .', 'My birthday party is going to be . . .' and so on.

 Low energy

Rhyming Nicknames

Put everyone's rhyming skills to the test

Age: 8 and up

Players: 2 and up

What you need: Nothing

How to play: One player announces the name of a (fictional) friend, and comes up with a biographical detail about them that rhymes with their name. Everyone else then takes it in turns to come up with another rhyme for them. For instance, the first player might say, 'I have a friend, her name is Eve. She likes to sew and knit and weave.' The next could chip in with 'She has a dog whose name is Steve', 'Her T-shirt has an orange sleeve', 'She's on a break in Tel Aviv' . . . anything that rhymes!

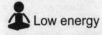 Low energy

501 *Throw more names around with Hot Talent [185].*

Rhyming Chain

A simpler alternative that doesn't require integrating rhyming words into a story. One person starts with a word, and everyone else, in turn, comes up with a word that rhymes with it. If they can't, they pass. Keep going until nobody can come up with any more, and the last player to come up with one gets to start the next round. You can keep score by getting 1 point every time you have to pass, with the lowest score winning.

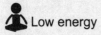 Low energy

The Alphabet Game

Make long car journeys zip by while trying to come up with a food beginning with X

Age: 8 and up

Players: 2 and up

What you need: Nothing

How to play: A category is chosen – countries! animals! famous people! – and going round from person to person, everyone names one thing in that category beginning with subsequent letters of the alphabet. Armenia! Belgium! Canada! If anyone really struggles, which is inevitable on some of the less-used letters of the alphabet, everyone else can help.

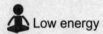 Low energy

Eternal Alphabet

Like the standard game, but instead of doing something beginning with A, then something beginning with B, then C, and so on, you use the last letter of the previous person's suggestion. Not only does this result in a game that can go on for a lot longer than 26 turns, it also means you don't know what your letter is until the person before you has had their go, meaning you can't plan ahead. A word of warning: most countries that begin with the letter A also end with the letter A, which can derail things immediately . . .

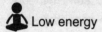 Low energy

Twenty Questions

Animal, vegetable or mineral?

Age: 8 and up

Players: 2 and up

What you need: Nothing

How to play: One player thinks of an object, animal or famous person and 'becomes' them. The other players then have up to 20 questions to figure out who or what they are. Obviously, none of the questions can be as blatant as 'Who or what are you?' – rather, hypothetical situations, either/or questions and gradual narrowing down are encouraged.

 Low energy

Tongue-Tied Twenty

All you can do is nod, shake your head, hold fingers up and shrug. This requires the players doing the asking to come up with some pretty creative questions.

 Low energy

Questions

Is this a game? Is it? Does anyone really know? What is a game? What is anything?

Age: 8 and up

Players: 2 and up

What you need: Nothing

How to play: Can you speak entirely in questions? Why not? It's a free country, isn't it? Is it, though? What do you mean by that? What do you think? What does – argh! Have as sensible a conversation as possible where everything anyone says is a question. Answering question upon question with further questions is deeply strange at first, but then it becomes easy enough, doesn't it?

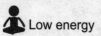 Low energy

Would You Rather . . . ?

An endless, winnerless, loserless game of hypothetical conundrums

Age: 8 and up

Players: 2 and up

What you need: Nothing

How to play: Take it in turns coming up with two hypothetical scenarios for everyone else to pick between. Would you rather never eat sweets again, or eat sweets for every meal for the rest of your life? Would you rather have an extra arm or an extra eye? Would you rather eat a whole jar of mayonnaise then go on a rollercoaster, or go on a rollercoaster and then have to eat a whole jar of mayonnaise? Justification of certain decisions can take vastly longer than anyone could reasonably expect.

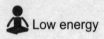 Low energy

Twenty-Second Treasure Trove

Deep-cut choices result in high scores

Age: 8 and up

Players: 2 to 6

What you need: A timer, paper and pencil to keep score

How to play: One category is decided that applies to everyone. Player one names as many things in that category as they can in 20 seconds, and scores 1 point for each one. Player two then gets 20 seconds to name as many as they can without repeating any of player one's, and gets 2 points for each, and so on. Play as many rounds as there are people, starting with a different person each time so everyone gets as many easy low-scoring starts as all-the-good-ones-are-gone high-scoring finishes.

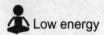 Low energy

In Common

The worlds of spelling and deduction collide

Age: 8 and up

Players: 3 and up

What you need: Nothing

How to play: One person thinks of an object and tells everyone else how many letters it has. If it's 'Cake', for instance, they'd say 'Four'. Then other players take it in turns suggesting words and are told how many letters they have in common with the secret object. So, a suggestion of 'Shoe' would get the answer 'one', while a suggestion of 'Bird' would get zero. By building on any that get positive scores (following 'shoe' with 'short', for instance, would get a score of 0, revealing the secret word had an E in it), and working together, you can gradually reveal the secret.

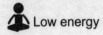 Low energy

Is It More Like . . . ?

When the sky is the limit, it's hard to know what to ask

Age: 8 and up

Players: 3 and up

What you need: Nothing

How to play: One player thinks of an object and, in as few questions as possible, everyone else has to figure it out by asking which of two things it's more like. As they can think of pretty much anything, you might end up with bizarre lines of questioning like 'Is it more like an apple or your Dad?' – a tricky question to answer if thinking about a car, for instance. It's inanimate, like an apple, but big, like your Dad . . . A big imagination and commitment to silliness definitely help in this one.

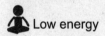 Low energy

Functions

Are you a mental maths machine?

Age: 8 and up

Players: 4 and up

What you need: Nothing

How to play: One player thinks up a mathematical function of some sort. It might be very straightforward, like 'add one', or it might be needlessly complicated 'squared, plus three, divided by two' – obviously everyone is encouraged to pick something appropriate to the other players' abilities. The other players take it in turns to say a number – the first player then tells them what their resulting number is after having the function applied to it. After one go around everyone, people have the option on their turn of suggesting a number or guessing the function.

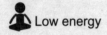 Low energy

Two Truths and a Lie

As personally insightful or strictly fact-based as you wish

Age: 8 and up

Players: Any number

What you need: Nothing

How to play: Everyone takes it in turns to say three statements about themselves, two of which are true and one of which is false. The other players have to work out, by talking with one another, which they think is the lie, delivering one answer between them. There's no winner as such, but everyone learns a bit about everyone else.

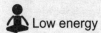 Low energy

Two Truths and a Tournament

The competitive version of Two Truths and a Lie. Everyone has a go, then all of the players who successfully misled the other players have another go, and all who are successful that time have another go, and so on until one person wins.

 Low energy

One-Minute Million

Speed, obscure knowledge and imagination combine with a time limit

Age: 8 and up

Players: Any number

What you need: A timer, paper and pencil to keep score

How to play: Take it in turns to name as many things from one particular category as you can in 60 seconds. Try to keep them as evenly matched as possible – if you're assigned the category 'food', don't then assign the next person 'directors of German Expressionist cinema'.

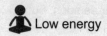 Low energy

Sixty-Second Subject

Inspired by a long-running radio series, can you speak for a minute without hesitation, repetition or deviation?

Age: 9 and up

Players: 3 and up

What you need: A timer

How to play: One person needs to act as a master of ceremonies. They give the players a subject, and begin the timer. The first player starts talking about the subject, while their opponents watch them like hawks. If they repeat themselves, go off-topic or end up just saying 'er' a lot, another player can 'buzz in' (which might just involve them shouting their name out), at which point the timer is paused. The buzzing player then explains what's happened, and if the master of ceremonies agrees, that player takes over the subject. The winner is whoever is talking when 1 minute is reached, even if they just started.

 Low energy

Crambo

An often-ridiculous rhyming game that requires quick thinking from everyone

Age: 9 and up

Players: 3 and up

What you need: Nothing

How to play: One player thinks of a word that has plenty of rhymes, and announces it by saying 'I'm thinking of a word that rhymes with _____'. The other players take it in turns to guess, but can't say the actual word they're guessing – they have to ask a question giving a clue as to what their guess is, which the first player has to figure out. For instance, if the word was 'book', the first player might say 'I'm thinking of a word that rhymes with look'. 'Is it something done with an oven?' 'No, it isn't cook.' 'Is it found on the end of a fishing line?' 'No, it isn't hook.' The game ends when the correct word is guessed or the guessers give up.

 Low energy

A Special List for a Special Day

Improvisation, deduction and imagined generosity – what a combo

Age: 9 and up

Players: 3 and up

What you need: Nothing

How to play: It is one player's birthday, and all the other players have bought them presents. However, there's a rule about what gifts are acceptable or not, and nobody's been told about it. The rule might be something like 'only blue presents', 'gifts made of gold' or 'all animals'. The celebrant begins by pretending to unwrap a perfect gift – one that meets the criteria – and tells everyone what it is. Guests at the party (the other players) then 'present' them with other pretend gifts, which are accepted or rejected with as much drama and gusto as feels right, while trying to figure out the rule.

 Low energy

Ghost

A difficult, compelling game for wordsmiths

Age: 10 and up

Players: 2

What you need: Nothing

How to play: The first player suggests a letter to begin a word, and then you take it in turns adding a letter but trying not to end up with a completed word. If you add a letter that can't actually form the beginning of a word, the other player can challenge you, and if you can't come up with an example, you lose. Each round finishes with a completed word or a successful or unsuccessful challenge. Whoever loses gets a letter of the word GHOST (like in the game Horse), and you play until someone has all five.

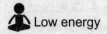 Low energy

El Fantasmo

One player begins a sentence with a word. The other player repeats it and adds another word. Go back and forth, repeating the whole lot each time and adding a new word to the sentence, until one player is unable to continue it or remember the sentence leading up to it.

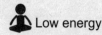 Low energy

Homophones

Fun with soundalikes

Age: 10 and up

Players: 2 and up

What you need: Nothing

How to play: One player comes up with a sentence that contains a pair of homophones – words with different meanings that sound the same. They then replace both of those words with another, unrelated word. So, 'I wonder whether the weather will be nice tomorrow' might become 'I wonder goblin the goblin will be nice tomorrow'. The other players then have to figure out what the missing pair of homophones is – whoever works it out does the next round. 'The umbrella neighed so loudly its throat went umbrella' is, obviously, about a horse. Right?

 Low energy

No More Dudes

A famous-people-naming game that quickly gets challenging

Age: 12 and up

Players: 2 and up

What you need: Nothing

How to play: Players take it in turns naming famous people
(of any kind) and adding a 'rule' that the person they just
named breaks. For instance, 'Scarlett Johansson. No more
people who've starred in Marvel movies.' 'Sir Francis Drake.
No more explorers.' 'Danny DeVito. No more people with
alliterative initials.' It all gets pretty difficult pretty quickly,
especially with enormous, sweeping rules like 'No more
dudes' or 'No more people who are currently alive.' Going
historical, obscure or fictional can help (until anyone brings in
rules like 'no more historical figures' and makes it hard again).

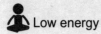 Low energy

Hot Talent

Can you figure out the mystery famous person just by throwing names around?

Age: 10 and up

Players: 2 and up

What you need: Nothing

How to play: One player thinks of a secret famous person. The other players take it in turns to suggest famous people, and after the first 'no', are only told whether subsequent suggestions are warmer (i.e. closer) or colder (further away) than the previous one. The aim is to figure out the big name within 20 guesses.

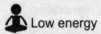 Low energy

501 *Keep the temperature theme going with Hot and Cold [13].*

185

Stinkety Pinkety

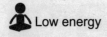

Cryptic clues for rhyming pairs

Age: 10 and up

Players: 2 and up

What you need: Nothing

How to play: Players take it in turns coming up with phrases made of two rhyming words and giving everyone else clues about them. For instance, 'A ship full of nannies and kids', 'A stallion that uses bad language' and 'A piece of furniture that never cheats' would work for 'goat boat', 'coarse horse' and 'fair chair'. Go as obscure and polysyllabic as you see fit, although good luck to anyone having to figure out that 'people born in an era where they look up to others' is 'veneration generation'.

 Low energy

Media Megastore

Searching your mental Netflix database

Age: 10 and up

Players: 2 and up

What you need: Nothing

How to play: One player chooses a subject (for instance, monkeys), and everyone then takes it in turns to name a film, book, game or song about that subject. If nobody else has heard of it, it doesn't count.

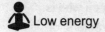 Low energy

Punlimited Entertainment

Instead of real titles, everyone comes up with jokey titles where real books, films and songs have had their names slightly changed to incorporate the theme. If the subject was 'monkeys', for instance, you might come up with The Apes Of Wrath, Good King Kong Wenceslas, The Wheels On The (Colo)Bus . . . Try to stick with things everyone will have heard of, and when nobody can think of any more, pick a new subject.

 Low energy

Celebrity Hangout

Can you embody an A-lister or fictional household name while simultaneously figuring out another's identity?

Age: 10 and up

Players: 3 and up

What you need: Pen and paper

How to play: One player is the adjudicator and timekeeper, and gives the other players little bits of paper with famous people's names on (which you can interpret or place limitations on however you want – depending on who is playing you could limit it to, say, fairytale characters, or characters from one particular TV show or book series). Those two players must then have a conversation for 1 minute, 'being' the person from their paper but without saying their names, while also trying to figure out the identity of the other 'famous person' they're talking to. The adjudicator interrupts if they feel anyone is being a bit too obvious. After the minute is up, players must name their famous friend.

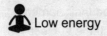 Low energy

Carnelli

A game of interconnected titles for bookworms, film buffs, music fans and pun enthusiasts

Age: 10 and up

Players: 4 and up

What you need: Nothing

How to play: One player starts off by saying the title of a film, book or song. The next has to come up with another that is somehow connected – it might be another work that has a lot in common with the first one, or one that has a word or two in common in its title. For instance, *The Lion King* could be followed up with the song 'The Lion Sleeps Tonight', or the film *King Kong*, or if you're a film buff you could go for another film by the same director . . . The next player then connects onto there – not onto the original title – and play continues. Players drop out if they can't think of anything, and the round is won by the last player standing.

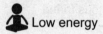 Low energy

Everyone From Everywhere Loves Everything

Like playing three alphabet games at once

Age: 10 and up

Players: Any number

What you need: Nothing

How to play: Going from person to person, everyone must introduce themselves, say where they're from and share a hobby, but each beginning with subsequent letters of the alphabet – for instance, 'I'm Alex, from Alaska, and I love angling' might be followed by 'I'm Boris, from Belgrade, and I love bowling.'

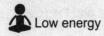 Low energy

Alice, Belgian Cellist

To make this hideously difficult, rather than your name, home and hobby all starting with the same letter, they need to start with subsequent ones. The first person has a name beginning with A, home beginning with B and hobby beginning with C, while the second has a name beginning with B, home beginning with C and hobby beginning with D.

 Low energy

Botticelli

A game of complicated answers to simple questions

Age: 12 and up

Players: Any number

What you need: Nothing

How to play: One person decides upon a famous person to embody and tells the other players the initial their name begins with. (Tradition dictates it has to be someone at least as well-known as the artist Sandro Botticelli, but it's the 2020s and *nobody* knows who that is – just ensure the person chosen is well-known enough that everyone will have a reasonable chance of working it out, and you know enough about them to answer questions 'as' them.) Another player then asks them questions, which they answer *as* that person, ideally eliminating one potential identity each time with a positive answer, and citing someone they aren't with a negative one. For instance, if you were Cristiano Ronaldo, you'd give the initial R and, if asked 'Are you an actor?', you'd reply 'No, I am not Ryan Reynolds'. If asked 'Are you a footballer?', you might reply 'Yes, but I am not Ronaldinho', placing the next player in a more knowledgeable position. If you can't think of a person to say that fits the initial and criteria, the person asking questions then gets to barrage you with yes/no questions, learning more about your identity until one results in the answer no. Then the next player starts grilling you, and so on.

 Low energy

Vermicelli

The same game, but made more delicious by replacing the famous person with food.

 Low energy

Looking Out the Window Games

I Spy, With My Little Eye

Observation, identification and transportation: what a combo!

Age: 7 and up

Players: 2 and up

What you need: Nothing

How to play: Take it in turns to pick something within view and introduce it by initial letter, with the preface 'I spy, with my little eye, something beginning with . . .' The other players can then ask questions about it – is it inside or outside? Is it rough or smooth? Is it a dark colour or a light colour? First to guess it wins.

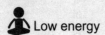 Low energy

I Spy With My Particularly Little Eye

Younger kids can play a variation where, instead of using letters, they can opt for sounds ('something beginning with ffffffffff'), colours ('something yellow' or even 'something the same colour as a lion') or shapes ('something shaped like a square').

 Low energy

Cryptic I Spy

Instead of giving an initial letter, go as mysterious as you can while still giving a clue. Rhyming clues ('I spy something that rhymes with free'), scientific clues ('I spy something that photosynthesises'), clues that rely on shared knowledge ('I spy something Granny has in her garden') or really challenging ones ('I spy something that is the beginning of what hospitals provide') can all work. (That's 'tree', by the way, as in 'tree-tment'.)

 Low energy

I Find, In My Clever Mind

An alternative to I Spy for when there isn't much to look at.

Age: 4 and up

Players: 7 and up

What you need: Nothing

How to play: Like I Spy, but for objects that aren't present. One player declares 'I find, in my clever mind, something beginning with . . .' and gives the first letter of an object they're thinking of. The other players quiz them on it – is this something we have in our house? Could you eat it? What does it feel like to touch? – and try to figure it out within 20 questions.

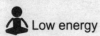 Low energy

Bus Stop

Age: 5 and up

Players: 2 and up

What you need: Nothing, but you need to be on a bus

How to play: On a bus journey, before each stop, everyone predicts how many people will get on at it and scores 1 point for every one they are wrong by – scoring works like golf, the lower the better. Use any clues you can – how busy the bus generally is, what time of day it is, whether you know the route and know you're approaching somewhere busy, just a gut feeling that it'll be two people – or just pluck a number from the air for fun, but you have to make your guesses before the stop is visible.

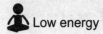 Low energy

Twinspotting

Age: 5 and up

Players: 2 and up

What you need: Nothing

How to play: Keep an eye out as you travel for pairs of anything – two buses passing one another, two blue cars next to each other, two buggies, two cows . . . Once you spot them, shout 'Twin [whatevers]!', and you get 1 point – once a pair has been claimed by one player, it can't be claimed by another. The first person to ten pairs wins.

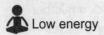 Low energy

The World is a Rainbow

Look, in order, for objects outside the car in every colour of the visual spectrum: red, orange, yellow, green, blue, indigo (let's call it navy blue) and violet (purple). An object can only be 'claimed' by one player, so getting started with that first red car is important. Orange and purple cars are pretty thin on the ground, so billboards are worth keeping an eye out for. The first player to complete the spectrum wins. If you like, you can play Mixed Rules, where a red car and a yellow car next to each other can be claimed as orange, and so on.

 Low energy

Letters in the Wild

Age: 5 and up

Players: 2 and up

What you need: Nothing

How to play: Looking out of the window, keep an eye out for the letter A. It might be on a number plate, on a signpost, a billboard, the road itself . . . When you spot it, point it out to everyone else and start looking for a B. Each letter in the outside world can only be claimed by one person, so there might be a real rush to claim the less-common letters like Q. Every player works their way through the alphabet, and the first to get to Z wins.

 Low energy

Wild World of Words

Just like Letters in The Wild, but instead of looking for the actual letter, players are looking for something beginning with that letter. You can be as imaginative as your fellow players will let you get away with – is 'quite tall person' acceptable as something starting with Q? How certain can anyone really be that the woman in the next car you're pointing to is a xylophonist?

 Low energy

Verbing

A game that only ends up sounding rude if you've got that sort of mind

Age: 6 and up

Players: 2 and up

What you need: Nothing

How to play: One player, the guesser, covers their ears while everyone else selects a verb (or, since covering ears isn't that effective, one other player chooses it, writes it down and shows it to everyone else). The guesser then has to figure it out by asking questions to every other player in turn, using the word 'verb' in its place. 'How often do you verb?', 'When was the last time you verbed?' 'Do you think I'm good at verbing?' and so on.

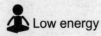 Low energy

Mine!

A simple but infuriating game of finders-keepers

Age: 6 and up

Players: 2 and up

What you need: Nothing

How to play: Collectively decide on one thing you're all trying to amass. Red cars, or cows, or traffic cones. Then, whenever you pass one, whoever shouts 'Mine!' first gets it. Whoever gets the most wins.

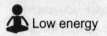 Low energy

Now!

One player secretly picks something that they're fairly confident they'll pass a lot of. Then, every time one of those things is passed, they announce 'Now!' The other players have to figure out what it is they are staking a claim to.

 Low energy

Three For a Pig

Accrue points by passing beasts

Age: 6 and up

Players: 2 and up

What you need: Nothing

How to play: Each player is assigned one side of the road (if more than two of you are playing, split into teams based on where you are sitting). Your goal is to score 100 points by observing animals as you pass them on your side of the road. Score 3 points for a pig (or, depending on where you are, an animal you can all agree you're fairly likely to see), 5 for any animal seen inside another vehicle, and 1 for any other non-human mammal you pass. If you go past a huge flock too large to count in the limited time you have, make a guess of up to 25.

 Low energy

Three For an Octopus

At the beginning of the journey, you get to pick which animals score you 3, and which lose you 10. However, this has to be approved by your opponent – you can't make things easier for yourself by going, 'Yeah, I guess I'm willing to sacrifice 10 points for every bear we pass.'

 Low energy

Three For a Freestyle Pig

Rather than limiting oneself to real animals, open up your options. Animals on pub signs, in place names, on billboards – anything. However, while imaginative options provide you with more opportunities for points, they also provide more opportunities to lose them, especially with a particularly observant, finickity opponent.

 Low energy

Counting Colours

Accrue massive scores over the course of a long journey

Age: 7 and up

Players: 2 and up

What you need: Nothing

How to play: Each player chooses a different colour. The aim is to score the most points by passing the most vehicles that are that colour, so if your favourite colours are fuchsia and ultramarine, you might want to think a little more practically. Score 1 point for a car that colour, two for a motorcycle, three for a van or lorry and five for a bus. Either play to 100 points or throughout the whole journey.

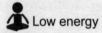 Low energy

Cursed Colours

Like Counting Colours, but every player starts on 100 points, and it is up to their opponents to knock points off their totals whenever relevant vehicles are passed. Can you distract the other players so much that they don't notice the fleet of yellow buses passing that would knock 60 points off your total?

 Low energy

Motorway Nemesis

Sorry, inhabitants of the silver 2001 Honda Civic in the outside lane: this time it's personal

Age: 8 and up

Players: 2

What you need: Nothing

How to play: When driving down a busy motorway, you often find yourselves travelling between the same two vehicles for ages. One player's nemesis is the vehicle in front, one is the vehicle behind. Score 2 points each for your nemeses turning on their lights or turning on their wipers, score 5 points if they change lanes and are no longer in the nemesis spot, and 10 points if they leave the motorway entirely. However, lose 5 points if the new nemesis that takes their place is the same colour, and 2 points if the new nemesis is bigger than the old one. Bonus point for every visible toy or animal. If in the same position for a long time, making up elaborate backstories about just how this car came to be your arch-enemy can be fun.

 Low energy

Service Station Scavenger Hunt

Make those all-too-necessary toilet stops a competitive part of the day

Age: 8 and up

Players: 2 and up

What you need: Pencil and paper

How to play: Spend some of your time on the road brainstorming what can be on your service station scavenger hunt. They don't need to be things you can bring back with you to the car, but one or two should. The rest can just be visual things you can see and tick off. A product reduction almost too good to resist. A picture of a coffee so large that, if it were life-size, whoever drank it would die. A ride based on a TV show. And so on . . .

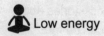 Low energy

The Colonel, the Clown and the King

Fast-food brands are massive, but which is the most massive?

Age: 8 and up

Players: 2 and up

What you need: Nothing

How to play: At the beginning of a long drive involving motorways, everyone in the car picks a different fast-food brand or chain cafe. As signs for service stations are passed, players score 1 point whenever the logo of their chosen chain shows up. Bonus point if it gets a whole sign to itself.

 Low energy

Nouns

A simple, wide-ranging, fast-paced, theoretically almost endless word game

Age: 8 and up

Players: 2 and up

What you need: Nothing

How to play: One at a time, going clockwise, everyone names an object beginning with the last letter of the one said by the person before them. There are a lot of objects in the world, obviously, so this can easily go on for absolutely ages, but the nature of it makes it all but impossible to plan ahead. One word of warning: a lot more objects end with E than start with it. Players drop out if completely stumped, and the last player standing wins.

 Low energy

Pub Cricket

Turns out you don't even have to go into a pub to enjoy it

Age: 8 and up

Players: 2 and up

What you need: Nothing

How to play: Pub Cricket is much more suited to driving through towns and countryside than long motorway journeys. Players are split into teams based on which side of the car they are sitting on, and score points based on pubs driven past. One point is scored for every leg mentioned in the pub's name – for instance, a pub called The Dog And Duck would score 6, while The King's Arms would score 0. If there is a non-specific plural in the name, such as The Coach And Horses, it counts as two horses and therefore 8 points.

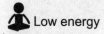 Low energy

Pub Test Match

Still in two teams, alternate who is 'at bat'. The team that is at bat accrues as many points as possible on both sides of the road, but are out if a pub is passed with 'Head' or 'Arms' in the name, and the other team bats. Keep a running total, and whoever has the most points when the game ends (when you get where you're going, when a certain time limit is reached or when both teams have had ten innings – whatever works) wins.

 Low energy

Number Plate Nicknames

Age: 8 and up

Players: 2 and up

What you need: Nothing but the view from the car window

How to play: Take it in turns coming up with nicknames for one another using the three letters at the end of the number plates of passing cars as initials. If a car passes with a plate ending in SMR, for instance, you might come up with Silly Master Robber, Smelly Monstrous Robot or Stupendously Magnificent Renegade.

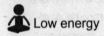 Low energy

Motorway Multiplex

Instead of nicknames for one another, use the initials on passing vehicles to come up with names for movies. Would you go and see Superman's Microscope Repair? What about Scary Moon Rollercoaster? Spider Munches Rocks? (What a film!)

 Low energy

Number Plate Baseball

Turn being stuck behind another vehicle into valuable points

Age: 8 and up

Players: 2 and up

What you need: Nothing

How to play: Form two teams. When one team is 'batting', they score points based on the number plate of the car in front. All of the numbers on the plate are added together, then multiplied by the number of vowels. For instance, EN51AJV would score 12 – 5 plus 1, and the vowels A and E. A team's time at bat ends when 0 is scored (due to a plate having no vowels), and the other team steps up to bat. Different number plate formats encountered while travelling can be both a blessing and a curse – the more numbers the better, but the fewer letters, the lower the likelihood of a vowel. Play until each team has been out nine times, and whoever has the highest score wins.

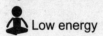 Low energy

Competitive Car Collecting

Who can amass the biggest automobile armada?

Age: 8 and up

Players: 2 and up

What you need: Nothing

How to play: Every player picks a group of vehicles –
depending on how much everyone knows/likes cars, you
might go for a colour (red/blue/grey), a manufacturer (Ford/
Nissan/Honda), a type (hatchback/van/motorcycle) or even an
ultra-specific model (Toyota Prius, etc). As you travel, keep an
eye out for anything in your category and keep a running total.

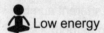 Low energy

Competitive Collecting Carousel

When playing on a very long journey, consider setting a
timer to go off every half-hour – when it goes off, everyone
rotates vehicle categories clockwise (i.e. replacing your
category with that of the person next to you).

 Low energy

Number Plate Encapsulate

Scour your internal dictionary for words containing whole plates of letters

Age: 10 and up

Players: 2 and up

What you need: Nothing

How to play: When a new vehicle appears in front of you, can you think of a word that includes all the letters on its number plate? One point if so, and a bonus point if all the letters appear in the word in the same order as on the plate.

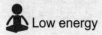 Low energy

Hand Games

Rock, Paper, Scissors

An ancient classic, perfect for making snap decisions or deciding who goes first in bigger games

Age: 6 and up

Players: 2

What you need: Nothing

How to play: Facing each other, say 'Rock, paper, scissors' in unison and hold your hand out, either as a clenched fist (a rock), a flat palm (paper) or making a scissor shape. Each beats one other option and in turn is beaten by another – scissors cut paper, paper wraps rock, rock breaks scissors.

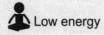 Low energy

Cow, Lake, Bomb

You can come up with endless variations of three things that work like rock, paper and scissors. For instance: cow, lake, bomb. A cow drinks a lake, the lake extinguishes a bomb, the bomb blows up a cow. Facing each other, say 'Cow, lake, bomb' in unison and then either moo, make a splashing sound or mimic an explosion. What else can you come up with? A frog eats a bee, the bee stings a person, the person eats a frog?

 Low energy

Rock, Paper, Nitwit

The actual winner is irrelevant in this deeply silly spin on Rock, Paper, Scissors, in which both players start with three lives. Instead of saying 'Rock, paper, scissors', players say 'Who's a nitwit?' When they both make their signs, the winner says 'You're the nitwit' and the 'loser' says 'I'm the nitwit'. If anyone gets this wrong, they lose a life. Winning each actual Rock, Paper, Scissors game is less important than adhering to the Nitwit Rules.

 Low energy

Odds and Evens

An instant-win game ideally suited to quick decision-making, like who gets the last doughnut

Age: 6 and up

Players: 2

What you need: Nothing

How to play: One player is Odd, one player is Even. At the count of three, both extend a number of fingers, from zero to ten. If the total presented between them is odd, Odd wins, and vice versa.

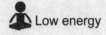 Low energy

Thumb War

A quick way to make a decision, or the seeds of an obsessively ongoing tournament

Age: 6 and up

Players: 2

What you need: Nothing

How to play: Players put their right hands together, keeping their fingers together and curling them around one another's similarly-curled fingers, their thumbs next to one another on the top. They chant 'One, two, three, four, I declare a thumb war' while criss-crossing their thumbs back and forth, and then the game is on – thumb-only wrestling, in which one player wins by pinning their opponent's thumb to the 'floor'.

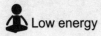 Low energy

Slaps

Less painful than it sounds, honest

Age: 6 and up

Players: 2

What you need: Nothing

How to play: Both players hold their hands out towards one another, palm down. One player puts theirs on top of their opponent's, almost but not quite touching. The player whose hands are underneath needs to bring their hands around to the top and tap the backs of their opponent's hands before they can bring their hands back out of the way. A successful dodge means swapping positions, and the first player to manage three successful taps in a row wins.

 Low energy

Hoi Sai

A Chinese hand game translating as 'all open'

Age: 6 and up

Players: 2

What you need: Pennies or counters as lives

How to play: The aim of this game is to correctly predict the total number of fingers you and your opponent will extend. Start with three lives each, and decide who is going first. Both players stand with their hands raised, fists clenched in front of their shoulders. The player whose turn it is shouts their prediction and both players extend their arms towards one another. Each hand can be presented as a closed fist (0) or an open palm (5), giving you the options of 'sau sai' ('all closed', i.e. 0), 5, 10, 15 or 'hoi sai' ('all open', i.e. 20). If you get it right, take a life and have another turn. If you get it wrong (which happens most of the time), return your hands to the start position – otherwise your opponent can have their turn and shout their prediction while looking at your hands!

 Low energy

> **501** *Fancy adding the element of wetness? Try Bucket Spoof [251].*

Chopsticks

Age: 6 and up

Players: 2

What you need: Nothing but fingers

How to play: Each player begins with their hands in front of them, in fists, with one finger extended on each. The object of the game is to eliminate both of your opponent's hands by getting them to the point where all five digits are extended by taking it in turns to tap one hand with another. Tapping one hand with another adds the amount of fingers on the first hand to the second hand, while the amount on the first hand stays the same – for instance, tapping your left hand against your right hand leaves you with one finger extended on your left and two on your right. When it's your turn, you can tap against your own hand or one of your opponent's hands. The number has to be exactly five to 'kill' a hand, though – if a hand with two fingers extended is tapped by one with four, for instance, it 'rolls over' to end up with one. The winner is the person who successfully eliminates both of their opponent's hands.

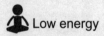 Low energy

Morra

A fast-paced Italian game where being able to count fingers quickly is a definite advantage

Age: 6 and up

Players: 3 or more

What you need: Nothing

How to play: Players stand in a circle and count 'One, two, three . . .' then put one hand forward into the circle, with between zero and five fingers extended, while shouting a number. The aim is to exactly guess the total number of fingers that will be shown – so, in a circle of five people, the maximum would be 25. If anyone says exactly the number, they get 1 point. First to 3 wins.

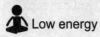 Low energy

Holiday Games

Find Some Fun: On Holiday

Use this high-tech, futuristic method to find a game to play, because why should you have to do all the work yourself?

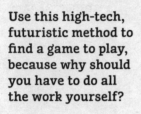

Are you on holiday?

Yes

No

Is there somewhere to swim?

Play Guggenheim [408] with some exotic travel-themed categories or I Packed My Bag [155] and pretend you are.

No

Yes

Enjoy the great outdoors with Frisbee Golf [145] or Wally [128]

So you're on the beach?

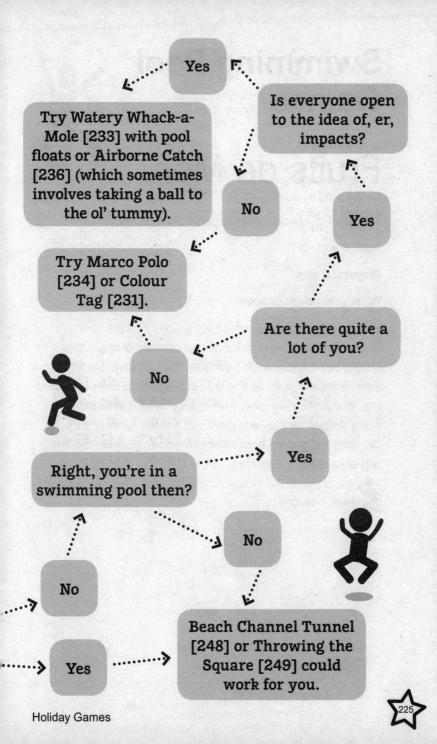

Yes

Is everyone open to the idea of, er, impacts?

Try Watery Whack-a-Mole [233] with pool floats or Airborne Catch [236] (which sometimes involves taking a ball to the ol' tummy).

No

Yes

Try Marco Polo [234] or Colour Tag [231].

Are there quite a lot of you?

No

Right, you're in a swimming pool then?

Yes

No

No

Beach Channel Tunnel [248] or Throwing the Square [249] could work for you.

Yes

Swimming Pool Games

Fruits de Mer

The most delicious a swimming pool will ever get

Age: 6 and up

Players: 2 to 4

What you need: Grapes

How to play: Throw a handful of grapes into the pool – unless you have purchased deeply unusual grapes, they should bob happily on the surface. Players take it in turns to swim from any point on the side of the pool to any other point in a straight line, keeping their eyes closed, gathering as many grapes as they can manage. Keep a running tally, throwing the grapes back after everyone's go, with the first player to reach 50 winning.

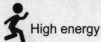 High energy

Speedy Seafood

Instead of doing one crossing of the pool, players get 10 seconds to gather as many grapes as they can. The timer starts when they hit the water and ends when they return 'home' (a designated point on the edge of the pool – the ladder works well). For every second over their 10, they lose 2 points.

 High energy

227

Beach Ball Bomb

If the ball touches the water, we're all in trouble!

Age: 6 and up

Players: 2 and up

What you need: A beach ball

How to play: That's no beach ball, it's a highly explosive, extraordinarily deadly device that reacts violently if it touches water. However, it also reacts violently if it stops moving. Keep batting it from one to another using your hands, never letting it touch the water lest ye all explode.

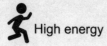 High energy

Airborne Alphabet

How long can you stay in mid-air? And how fast can you talk?

Age: 6 and up

Players: 2 and up

What you need: Nothing

How to play: Take it in turns jumping into the swimming pool and reciting as much of the alphabet as you can before hitting the water. You can't start speaking until your feet leave the ground. The player who manages to complete the alphabet in the fewest jumps wins.

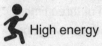 High energy

Airborne Interrogation

A combination of Twenty Questions [170] and gravity, this involves sharing information while plummeting towards the water's surface. One player assumes the identity of something or other. Their opponent jumps into the pool, counting as many questions as they can – 'One question, two questions, three questions, SPLASH!' They can then ask that many questions, calmly, by the side of the pool. However, questions can only be answered in the air – 'Yes, Dougie, no, SPLASH!'

Submarine Karaoke

Singing underwater – how all the greats started out

Age: 6 and up

Players: 3 and up

What you need: Nothing

How to play: Take it in turns to be the singer. Everyone goes underwater and the singer sings or hums as much of a song as they can. If anyone figures it out they give a big thumbs-up and everyone surfaces to hear their guess. If it's right, both the guesser and singer get 1 point. If it's wrong, everyone goes underwater to hear it again (a maximum of three times) and no points are scored. Make sure to use songs everyone knows, and play until one person gets to 5 points.

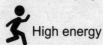 High energy

Deep Voices

Guessers wait in the pool while the singer runs up and jumps in – they can start singing in the air and continue underwater (NB this transition can be a bit, um, chlorine-y) as the guessers lower their heads beneath the surface. The singers have to surface naturally (i.e., they can't swim to keep themselves under longer), and guessers raise their hands upon resurfacing.

 High energy

Colour Tag

Stealthy swimming

Age: 6 and up

Players: 4 and up

What you need: Nothing

How to play: One player is It and stands outside the pool with their back to it. The other players start at the other end of the pool, and each of them assign themselves a colour. It doesn't matter if multiple players have the same colour. Then It starts calling out colours. If your colour is called, you have to get to the other end of the pool without being seen moving when/if It turns around. If It suspects people are moving, they can turn around, and if everyone is still – even if they're halfway up the pool – It has to take a step further away from the pool. If a player is seen moving, though, It can jump into the pool, whereupon it becomes a free-for-all of people trying to get to the end without being tagged. If a player is tagged, they become It. Anyone who makes it to the end of the pool without being tagged scores a goal. Most goals by the time everyone's tired wins.

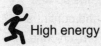 High energy

Octopus Alert

What maniac let an octopus into the swimming pool?

Age: 6 and up

Players: 4 and up

What you need: Nothing

How to play: One person is the octopus and goes in the middle of the pool, while the other players line up at one end. On a signal, they all try and get to the other end of the pool without being tagged by the octopus (by linking arms with them). Anyone who is tagged becomes part of the octopus, which gradually becomes a multi-headed, many-limbed, ever so wide beast that occasionally struggles to only move in one direction.

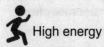 High energy

501 *Fancy getting wet but don't have a swimming pool to hand? Hosepipe Limbo [136] is what you're after.*

Watery Whack-a-Mole

A game of gentle aquatic impacts

Age: 6 and up

Players: 6 and up

What you need: A float, a timer

How to play: One player is the Whacker. They stand in the pool, and the other players surround them in a circle. The players in the circle go underwater, trying to surface when the Whacker is facing the other way – whenever anyone's head bobs above the surface, the Whacker can (lightly) bonk them on the head with the float. The Whacker has 1 minute and scores 1 point per bonk before swapping with another player, who becomes the new Whacker.

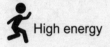 High energy

Marco Polo

Celebrate global exploration pretty locally

Age: 7 and up

Players: 3 and up

What you need: Nothing

How to play: One player is 'Marco' and must close their eyes and loudly count to ten as the other players disperse around the pool. Keeping their eyes closed, Marco shouts 'Marco!', at which point the other players must respond 'Polo!' Marco then tries to tag people by following their voices, shouting as frequently as they need to, although everyone is allowed to keep moving. If Marco tags someone, they become Marco and the game begins again. Or, if Marco suspects that one of the players has got out of the pool, they shout 'Fish out of water!' – if they're right, the mantle is passed.

 High energy

Silent Ships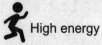

In a pool shallow enough to walk around in, one player who is 'It' counts to ten as everyone else disperses. Keeping their eyes closed, they then walk around the pool trying to corner and tag people, while everyone tries to evade capture as silently as possible.

 Low energy

Sunken Treasure

One for confident underwater swimmers

Age: 8 and up

Players: 2 to 4

What you need: A handful of coins

How to play: Throw a handful of assorted coins into the pool. Players take it in turns seeing how much money they can gather in one dive, working towards a certain target – say, three pounds. The coins are thrown back in after every dive, and whoever reaches the target first wins.

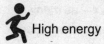 High energy

Cursed Treasure

Designate certain denominations as 'evil' – if a diver returns with one of those among their haul, they score 0 for that go. This means players can't just blindly grab everything they can, and have to plan their dives a little better.

 High energy

Airborne Catch

Catching things while mid-air above a pool is just about as cool as anyone ever gets to look

Age: 8 and up

Players: 2 and up

What you need: Any bits and bobs that can be thrown and caught – balls, pool toys, goggles, anything really

How to play: Split into teams of two. Teams take it in turns to do as much airborne catching as they can in one jump: one person jumps from the side of the pool while their teammate throws things at them from wherever they want – as many things, thrown one at a time or together, it's up to them. Score 2 points for everything caught but lose 1 point for everything missed, so be wary of going too overambitious. Swap places every round, so everyone both throws and catches, and the first team to 25 points are the winners.

 High energy

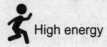

Keep My Luggage Dry

To add an extra level of difficulty, players not only have to catch objects while in the air, they have to keep them out of the pool. Raising arms, instantly treading water and generally trying not to end up with half the pool up your nose are all advised. How fastidious teams wish to be about awarding points if things get splashed is up to them.

 High energy

Sharks and Minnows

Underwater skills and great timing are key to beating the Great Whites

Age: 8 and up

Players: 4 and up

What you need: Nothing

How to play: In a swimming pool, select one player as the shark. They start on the opposite side of the pool from the rest of the players, who are minnows. In each round, the minnows must swim from one side of the pool to the other without being tagged by the shark while above the surface of the water. Any minnow who is tagged above the water's surface joins the shark for the next round. Play until only one minnow, powerful ruler of all minnowkind, remains.

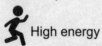 High energy

501 *Not near water? Play a drier version of this with British Bulldog [270].*

The Sinker

Unbearable suspense followed by explosive splashes

Age: 8 and up

Players: 5 and up

What you need: A selection of objects, some buoyant, some not, that could be easily retrieved with one hand

How to play: One player at a time is the Sinker. All other players stand along the edge of the pool with their backs to it. The Sinker chooses an object from the selection and either throws it into the pool, delicately places it there or goes in with it, leaving it somewhere along the way. None of the other players can turn around to see what the Sinker has chosen or where it is, but they can listen away. From outside the pool, the Sinker shouts 'Go!' and the others have to figure out what the object is and where it is, and get it before their rivals do. Whoever gets it first is the next Sinker.

 High energy

Almost Volleyball

Who needs an actual net?

Age: 8 and up

Players: 6 and up

What you need: A ball, two chairs

How to play: Put a chair on either side of the pool at the halfway point – this is where your imaginary net is, at the level of the outside of the pool. Form two teams, one on each half of the pool. The aim is to get the ball into the water on your opponent's side of the net while avoiding it hitting the water on your side, but catching isn't allowed – players can only hit the ball with their hands. The ball has to be in the air when it crosses the 'net line'. Boosting a teammate out of the pool for impressive aerial manoeuvres isn't just allowed, it's very much encouraged. In a pool with a shallow end and deep end, swap after every point. First to 10 wins.

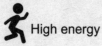 High energy

Not Quite Polo

Put the chairs at either end of the pool instead – these are goals. Without travelling with the ball, the aim is to score points by getting the ball into the opposing team's goal by passing, intercepting it and generally working well as a team.

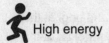 High energy

Splash!

Suspense-filled poolside fun

Age: 8 and up

Players: 6 and up

What you need: A bucket, paper and pen

How to play: Get one more piece of paper than there are players, write numbers on them (so, if you have seven players, write 1 to 8 on different pieces of paper) and put them in a bag. One player reaches in and secretly looks at one. They then stand holding a bucket of water, with everyone else surrounding them in a circle. They point at each other player in turn, who has to say a number – one that hasn't been said yet. When someone says the number the person in the centre saw, they're allowed to throw the bucket of water into their face. You can throw it as soon as they say the number ('ThreeSPLASHargh!'), but another fun way of adding to the surprise is to act like you're moving on to the next person and catching them off guard. If nobody says the number, the person in the middle has to pour the bucket over their own head.

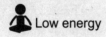 Low energy

Chickenfight

Piggybacks plus water equals horseplay

Age: 12 and up

Players: 4
What you need: Nothing

How to play: In a swimming pool, form teams of two, with the smaller team member sitting on the shoulders of the larger one. The shoulder-riders then attempt to wrestle one another off and into the pool – no hitting, of course, just grappling.

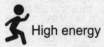 High energy

Chicken in the Middle

You need six people and a ball for this – a double-decker, aquatic version of Piggy in the Middle. The people sitting on shoulders handle the ball, the people below handle the movement. In a big enough pool, the lower piggy may choose to 'launch' the higher piggy to intercept the ball.

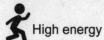 High energy

Beach Games

Pooh Sticks

As popularised by literature's favourite little-brained bear

Age: 4 and up

Players: 2 and up

What you need: A stick each

How to play: Pooh Sticks requires being on a footbridge or pier. Players get a stick each and drop them from the upstream side of the bridge, then cross over to the downstream side and see whose stick comes out first.

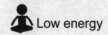 Low energy

Leaky Lifesaver

Wet heads for everyone!

Age: 5 and up

Players: 2 and up

What you need: A water bottle each, with a hole punched in the bottom, buckets

How to play: Making a hole in the bottom of the bottles can be a bit tricky – a corkscrew can come in handy (this is a job for grown-ups). Players have to fill their buckets by carrying water, a bottleful at a time, from the pool or sea. The thing is, they have to hold the bottles above their heads while doing so. The first to fill their bucket wins.

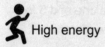 High energy

> **501** *Have slightly drier bucket-based fun with Balls in the Bucket [400].*

Pebble Petanque

Aka 'Budget Beach Boules'

Age: 6 and up

Players: 2 to 4

What you need: Five decent-sized and vaguely symmetrical pebbles, a stick to draw

How to play: Smooth out an area of sand, and draw three concentric circles and a line to stand behind – use your own judgement on distances based on who's playing, but 3 or so metres away is a good start. Take it in turns to stand behind the line and, using underarm throws, toss stones towards the circles, trying to score as many points as possible. Score 20 points in the smallest circle, 10 for the middle one and 5 for the biggest. The player with the highest score after five turns wins.

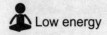 Low energy

Castle Cannon

Carefully build a sandcastle then watch as your opponent mercilessly destroys it

Age: 6 and up

Players: 2 and up

What you need: Buckets, spades, a small stick per person (lolly sticks are ideal), pebbles

How to play: Everyone builds a sandcastle, all equal distances from one another, and places a stick in the top. Then, players take it in turns to throw stones at each other's castles from behind their own, aiming to knock the sticks out. Players whose sticks are knocked out can no longer throw, so if playing with more than two people, it's worth thinking tactically about who you want to take out . . .

 Low energy

Beach Channel Tunnel

Seaside engineering: a game today, a millionaire-making career tomorrow

Age: 6 and up

Players: 2 and up

What you need: A tennis ball each, a spade (optional)

How to play: From the same starting point, everyone has 15 minutes to build a track to the sea for a tennis ball to roll down. All the balls are then released at once. If a ball stops or comes out of a track, the player whose ball it is has to run down and reset it. The winner is the player whose ball gets to the sea first.

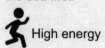 High energy

Slow But Steady

Build tracks, but try to make them as long and meandering as possible while ensuring balls will still roll down them. Roll balls down the tracks one at a time, timing them. Every time you need to go and give your ball a push to get it going again, knock 2 seconds off your time. The engineer with the longest time wins.

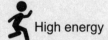 High energy

Throwing the Square

An old Chinese game perfectly suited to the beach

Age: 6 and up

Players: 2 and up

What you need: A stick to draw in the sand with, flat pebbles or pieces of driftwood

How to play: Draw two squares in the sand next to one another, about 30cm each. Draw another line about 2 metres away for players to stand behind. The first player throws their stone into one of the squares (and can have another go if they miss – they can't score any points anyway), then every other player stands behind the line and tries to get their stone into the same square. Getting it into the same square scores 2 points, the other square scores 1, and missing the squares entirely scores 0. Rotate who does the first throw (as that player can't score), and the first to 10 wins.

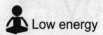 Low energy

Buried Legs Olympics

Everything is that bit more challenging when half of your body is below ground

Age: 8 and up

Players: 4 and up

What you need: Buckets and spades, a ball

How to play: Form teams of two – the buried athlete and the executive sand assistant. Dig a hole in the sand big enough for the athlete to sit in and bury their legs. Buried players now have to compete in tasks put together by their assistants. Who can throw the ball furthest? Who can land it in a faraway bucket the most times in a row? Who can have the most buckets of water poured over their heads without complaining?

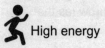 High energy

Bucket Spoof

A tournament you want to get kicked out of as soon as possible.

Age: 8 and up

Players: Any number

What you need: Three coins, stones or counters each, plus a bucket

How to play: Everyone stands in a circle and extends a closed fist containing between zero and three counters. The first player guesses how many total counters they think there are, followed by the second player, and so on. Nobody can guess a number someone else has already guessed. When everyone has guessed, all hands are opened and counters revealed. If anyone guessed precisely, they are out (it's good to be out). The next player clockwise begins the next round. Play until only one person is left, at which point everyone in turn gets to empty a bucket of water over their head.

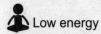 Low energy

501 *If it's wet heads you're into, have a go at Soak the Adult [284].*

International Bucket Spoof

At the elite level of International Bucket Spoof, extra rules apply. Counters must be extended in the left hand, and play goes anticlockwise. Every player who successfully escapes the game gets to instil another rule – unbreakable laws, like saying numbers in Spanish, jumping up and down while making your prediction, and replacing the number 3 with a rude noise have all been known. Anyone breaking the rules, whether deliberately or accidentally, gets half a bucket of water poured over their rebellious heads.

 Low energy

Crab Football

A bent-over-backwards, beachy version of the Beautiful Game

Age: 10 and up

Players: 6 and up

What you need: A beach ball, a decent amount of space

How to play: Shoes off, space cleared, and then it's the usual rules of football, except that everyone's hands are on the floor behind them, and they scuttle like crabs. Also, no goalkeepers. Just to repeat, shoes off. This one can get pretty hairy, and faces aren't as far away from feet as they would usually be. Shoes off! SHOES OFF!

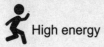 High energy

Party and Big Group Games

Find Some Fun: At A Party

Use this high-tech, futuristic method to find a game to play, because why should you have to do all the work yourself?

Are you all boisterous and full of energy?

Yes

No

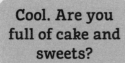

Cool. Are you full of cake and sweets?

Kim's Game [318] or Fish and Chips [356] are nice and chilled to pass the time until you get all riled up and bonkers.

No

Yes

Well, put that right with Dangling Doughnuts [307] or Sweet, Sweet Memories [315].

Is the weather nice enough to go outside?

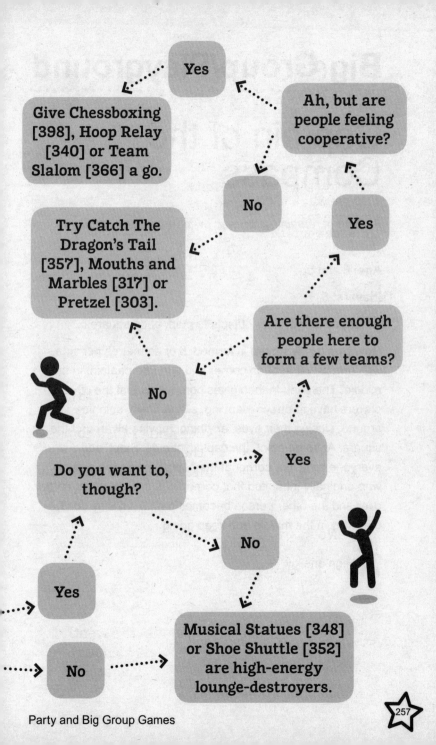

Yes

Give Chessboxing [398], Hoop Relay [340] or Team Slalom [366] a go.

Ah, but are people feeling cooperative?

No

Yes

Try Catch The Dragon's Tail [357], Mouths and Marbles [317] or Pretzel [303].

Are there enough people here to form a few teams?

No

Do you want to, though?

Yes

No

Yes

No

Musical Statues [348] or Shoe Shuttle [352] are high-energy lounge-destroyers.

Big Group/Playground

Captain of the Compass

A game of remaining focused even when asked to be very silly

Age: 6 and up

Players: 5

What you need: Four objects to mark out a square

How to play: A square is formed, 8 or so metres per side, with one player in each corner and one (the captain) in the middle. The captain then gives commands that the other players have to obey – dancing, sitting down, spinning around, closing their eyes, anything, moving all around the square. At some point, the captain shouts 'Stop!' and everyone runs to a corner. If the captain beats the person who originally inhabited that corner to it, they take that corner over and the other person becomes captain. If they don't, they stay in the middle and keep going.

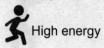 High energy

Tag

A never-ending game of passing it on

Age: 6 and up

Players: 6 and up

What you need: Nothing

How to play: One player is It, and runs after everyone else trying to tag them. When someone is tagged, they are now It and the original one isn't any more. There is no defined end point – play until everyone's tired.

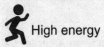 High energy

Shadow Tag

Instead of tagging people physically, jump into their shadow to tag them. This variation obviously works better at certain times of day and certain times of year.

 High energy

Octopus Tag

When It tags someone, they latch on and hold hands, and keep trying to tag more people. It ends up longer and longer and longer, but teamwork is required to all run in the same direction.

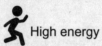 High energy

Amoeba Tag

Like Octopus Tag, except all the Its have to form a circle and figure out how to move in one direction together.

 High energy

Hospital Tag

This variation requires a lot more Its from the get-go (try with one It for every two non-Its), and being tagged a lot more times, being 'injured' stage by stage. After being tagged the first time, hold your elbows in your opposite hands. After being tagged a second time, put your hands on your knees. When tagged a third time, lie down and 'die'. Last person alive wins.

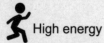 High energy

Party and Big Group Games

Half-Tag

Similar to Hospital Tag, but after being tagged once, players have to hop. Then, when tagged again, they become It.

 High energy

Pair Tag

Normal Tag, but people can only be tagged if they're on their own – if you form a pair with someone (by holding hands with them), you are untaggable. However, you can only be paired with that person for 5 seconds, after which you have to let go and make a break for it.

 High energy

Bally Hey

Like regular Tag, but It tries to pass its It-ness on by throwing a tennis ball at people. Gently, obviously.

 High energy

Ankle Tag

An extremely loud, destructive variation on tag

Age: 6 and up

Players: 6 and up

What you need: Balloons, string

How to play: Everyone ties an inflated balloon to their right ankle, apart from one person, who is It. It needs to tag people by popping their balloons, at which point they join them and also try to pop other people's balloons. The last person with an intact balloon wins.

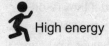 High energy

Stuck in the Mud

Tag with a swampy difference

Age: 6 and up

Players: 6 and up

What you need: Nothing

How to play: One person (or more in a big group) is It, and runs around trying to tag people. When tagged, they are stuck in the mud, and have to stand still with their arms stretched out to their sides and their legs apart. Someone who is stuck in the mud can only be released by another player crawling under their legs. Keep going until everyone's stuck, or if that's not happening, add some more Its.

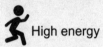 High energy

Hug in the Mud

Crawling under other people's legs isn't everyone's cup of tea, especially if actual mud is involved, so if nobody fancies wriggling around on the floor trying to free people, replace crawling under legs with a friendly, freeing hug.

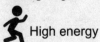 High energy

Qiu

Named after the Chinese word for 'ball', this traditional game would be played using all the children from a village

Age: 6 and up

Players: 10 and up

What you need: A ball

How to play: Everyone forms a circle, and the ball is thrown across it from person to person. Whenever someone catches the ball, the players on either side of them raise the arm closest to them. If you fail to catch the ball (unless it was an undeniably bad throw), forget to raise your arm or raise the wrong one, you are out. The five players who stay in the game the longest are joint winners.

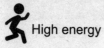 High energy

Non-Stop Cricket

A fast-paced, equipment-light version of the longest sport in the world

Age: 7 and up

Players: 10 and up

What you need: One set of 'stumps' (easily enough improvised with a pile of cans or other household items), a bat, a ball, a cone or something similar to mark the bowling spot

How to play: Split into two teams – batters and fielders. Batters line up beside the stumps, while the fielders spread out. One fielder bowls underarm from the bowling spot (but every six balls, the bowler changes). The batter has to run whether they hit the ball or not, go around the bowling spot and back to their stumps – that is one run. Fielders try to get the ball back to the bowler, who can bowl even if the batter is nowhere near ready. Batters try to score as many runs as possible. They are out if the stumps are hit, whether by the bowler or a fielder stumping them out while running. When out, batters pass the bat to the next player until the whole team is out. However, if a player is caught out, the whole team is out, their innings are over and teams swap places. Play as many innings as you wish, with the highest-scoring team winning the day.

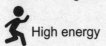 High energy

Smugglers

Learn how to get contraband across international borders. Wait, no, don't!

Age: 7 and up

Players: 20 and up

What you need: A few pieces of paper to function as 'contraband' – ideally impossible to fake more of, so something like a signature from an authority figure might help, plus bibs or bands to identify teams

How to play: Split into two teams. One team are smugglers, the other are customs. One area is designated 'home' – this is where the smugglers are trying to get their contraband to. Any customs agent can tag any smuggler. If tagged by customs, smugglers have to let themselves be searched, so they need to work together and make plans – do they go for really clever hiding places? Or do they use red herrings, sending obvious suspects in to get the attention of customs while the real smuggler sneaks in quietly? After fifteen minutes, if fewer than half of the contraband items have made it home, customs wins.

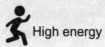 High energy

Duck Hunt

You don't have to dress up as a duck for this, but it can't hurt, can it?

Age: 8 and up

Players: 8 and up

What you need: Tennis balls, a timer

How to play: One area is designated 'the pond'. Three metres away is 'the bank'. Split into two teams, ducks and hunters – ducks go into the pond, hunters stand on the bank. The hunters aim to hit the ducks below the knee with tennis balls, while the ducks aim to stay un-hit as long as possible. Go for about half as many balls as there are hunters. Hits above the knee don't count. Hunters can run into the pond to retrieve balls, but can only throw them from the bank. When a duck is hit, they leave the pond. Play until all ducks have been hit, then swap over – the new team of ducks have a time to beat.

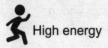 High energy

Mega Duck Hunt

Instead of ducks who have been hit having to leave the pond, they stay on, but with every hit recorded. Play for 3 minutes, with hunters aiming to hit the ducks as many times as possible and ducks doing their best to avoid being struck.

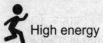 High energy

Crack the Whip

An extremely fast game best played on forgiving ground

Age: 8 and up

Players: 8 and up

What you need: Nothing

How to play: Players stand in a row holding hands. The player at one end is the head of the whip, and starts running around, bringing everyone else with them. If the head turns tight corners, the people at the back of the whip can suddenly find themselves travelling extremely fast and going flying everywhere. Players who fall off can try to reattach themselves – potentially moving up a few places in the process if others have fallen off too – and try to stay attached for as long as possible.

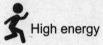 High energy

British Bulldog

End-to-end stuff with loads of international variations

Age: 8 and up

Players: 10 and up

What you need: Nothing

How to play: Play on a large, designated area – a clearly marked rectangle like a courtyard or garden is ideal. One or two players are chosen to be the Bulldogs, and stand in the middle of the playing area with everyone facing them from one end. One Bulldog shouts 'British Bulldog, one, two, three!', at which point all the other players try to run to the other end of the playing area, while the Bulldogs try to tag them. Everyone tagged becomes a Bulldog too, and the ratio of runners to dogs shifts and shifts.

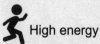 High energy

501 *Enjoying exploring your canine side? Be a full-on animal in Hunter and Guard [276].*

Hopping Jinny

Hopping Jinny is a slightly silly variation where everyone hops at all times with their arms folded across their chests. Bulldogs convert runners by shoulder-barging them and making them put their other foot down.

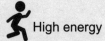 High energy

Bullrushes

A British Bulldog variation that allows for tactical targeting, where a head start is not an advantage

Age: 8 and up

Players: 10 and up

What you need: Nothing

How to play: Start off like British Bulldog, with everyone at one end of the playing area except for one person in the middle. However, rather than making a call that leads everybody to run, they can name individuals, for example: 'Bullrush . . . Mabel!' Mabel then has to start on her own, with everyone else only running 2 seconds after her.

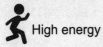 High energy

Team Bullrush

Players form pairs or groups of three and give themselves team names – Team Ramrod, Axe United, whatever – and are called out by team name. 'Bullrush . . . The Idiots!'

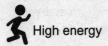 High energy

Chilly Dogs

Instead of tagged players becoming regular Bulldogs, they have to freeze totally still where they are tagged. Bulldogs can then try to corral other players towards them, where they can be tagged – after a while the playing area can become like an obstacle course.

 High energy

Two-Headed Bulldog

This method can get complicated as you have people running from both ends.

Age: 8 and up

Players: 10 and up

What you need: Nothing

How to play: Rather than calling for everyone or singling out individuals, the Bulldog in this variation goes trait-based, calling out groups by things like clothing, hair colour, or more offbeat groupings such as which half of the year they were born. 'People in blue trousers . . . Bulldog!' Fairly swiftly, people will be running in both directions on every run, criss-crossing in the middle and adding another element (trying not to run into one another) into the mix.

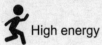 High energy

Cops and Robbers

Law enforcement, playground style

Age: 8 and up

Players: 10 and up

What you need: Nothing

How to play: One section of the playing area is designated 'Jail'. Half the players are cops and half are robbers. The cops run around trying to catch the robbers and take them to jail – when a robber is caught, they have to go with the cop – and if they manage to imprison them all, the game is over and justice has been done. However, robbers can free jailed robbers by high-fiving them. What's more, while jailed robbers can't leave jail, they can stretch out as far as they can in human chains in order to make freedom more likely.

 High energy

Kick the Can

A can is placed in the middle of the playing area, and instead of being freed by high-fiving, prisoners can only be freed if a robber kicks the can over. Whenever it is kicked over, everyone being held in jail is free.

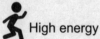 High energy

Capture the Flag

Like video games, but real!

Age: 8 and up

Players: 10 and up

What you need: Two similar things to act as 'flags' – cones, jackets, anything that is fairly visible

How to play: Each team has a base with their flag in and a designated 'jail' space. The object of the game is to steal the other team's flag from their base and bring it to your own, but if caught, you can be imprisoned in the other team's jail (attached to their base). One of your teammates can free you by coming in and tagging you, but you then have to return to your own base before trying to steal the flag.

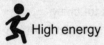 High energy

Hunter and Guard

A wide game with a jail

Age: 8 and up

Players: 10 and up

What you need: Some way of marking out a circle

How to play: One player is a hunter, one is a guard, and the rest are animals. A pen is marked out for the guard to stay in – a circle 4 or so metres in diameter is ideal, or pre-existing boundaries and areas can be used. The guard stays in this area for the whole game, while the hunter goes out catching animals, who try to hide and/or outrun the hunter. When an animal is tagged by the hunter, they accompany them back to the pen, where the guard keeps hold of them. Other animals can release trapped ones by sneaking in and touching them – but doing so of course puts them at high risk of getting tagged by the guard. Play until five animals are trapped in the pen – that's plenty for the hunter and guard to start their own zoo with.

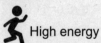 High energy

501 *Into hunting, are you? Test your abilities with The Great Sock Hunt [22].*

Party and Big Group Games

I Am Not a Number

A game best played across a wide area involving a lot of inter-team communication

Age: 8 and up

Players: 12 and up

What you need: Cards or paper plates, numbered 1 to 11

How to play: Hide the numbers around a designated area beforehand – the bigger the better. They should be hidden, but in a way that doesn't require them to be touched for the numbers to be seen. Split players into two teams. One will start from 1, and the other from 11. Players then have to work within their teams to get as many cards as possible and bring them back to the starting point. The thing is, cards are only 'unlocked' when one to either side of them is found, i.e. you can't pick up the number 3 card if you find it until you've worked your way up (or down) to it. Teams need to form plans to explore the area and check in with one another to exchange information and retrieve what they can. The team that returns number 6 – after returning either 1 to 5 or 11 to 7, of course – wins.

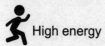 High energy

Reject This False World

Instead of numbers, hide the letters of a password, eight to ten letters long. Tell everyone how many letters there are, but not what it is. Teams then have to find the letters and rearrange them into a word. The first team to return to the starting point and tell you the password wins. However, the whole team needs to be present to tell you it, and if they get it wrong, they all have to stay at the starting point for 1 minute while the other team keeps exploring. There's plenty of room for guesswork – a few key letters might give it away – but also plenty for mistakes.

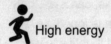 High energy

French Cricket

Not French, and not a lot like cricket

Age: 9 and up

Players: 6 and up

What you need: A tennis ball and something to hit it with – ideally a cricket bat or tennis racquet, but feel free to improvise and get a wooden rolling pin involved

How to play: The batter stands in the middle of a big circle of fielders. The player facing the batter throws the ball, trying to hit the batter below the knee. The batter tries to hit the ball away and prevent their legs – the stumps – being hit. If the stumps are hit, the batter is out. If they hit the ball and it's caught before bouncing, they are out. The next fielder clockwise bowls the next ball, but the batter can only move their feet if they hit the ball – otherwise they have to twist around to protect their stumps. The batter scores 1 point for every bowl they survive, and whoever bowls or catches them out swaps in to bat.

 High energy

501 *Keep the bat in your hand with a game of Minimalist Rounders [394].*

Break the Gates

A fairly physical game for older players

Age: 10 and up

Players: 10 and up

What you need: Nothing

How to play: Form two teams, each of which stands in a row holding hands. Teams face one another from about 3 metres apart. Each team takes it in turns to send one player to 'break the gates' by running towards the other team and trying to force their way through one of the links. If they succeed, the players on each side go back with them and join the other team. If they fail, they stay and join that team. Keep playing until one team is down to two players – if that link breaks, everyone's on the same team and the game is over.

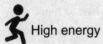 High energy

Red Rover

Very similar, except the choice of who goes is made by the opposing team, who chant 'Red rover, red rover, let [their name] come on over!' If they succeed, they take the two players at the broken link back with them. If they fail, they join that team at the point they tried to break it.

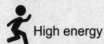 High energy

Party Games

Pass the Parcel

A beloved combination of music and property acquisition

Age: 3 and up

Players: 6 and more

What you need: A present, wrapped in multiple layers of wrapping paper

How to play: Everyone sits in a circle and some music is put on. The present is passed from person to person until the music stops, at which point the person holding it removes one layer. Keep playing until someone finishes unwrapping the present, which they get to keep. Some people opt to put smaller gifts or sweets between every layer, and if whoever is in charge of the music is on the ball, that can even be pre-planned.

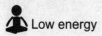 Low energy

Pass the Panama

Fill a bag or basket with dressing-up clothes, hats and silly accessories. Sit everyone in a circle, like Pass The Parcel, and put music on. When the music stops, whoever is holding the basket has to put something on. Get two or three baskets going around larger groups and everyone will look ridiculous in no time at all.

 Low energy

Hide and Seek

An age-old perennial

Age: 4 and up

Players: 3 and up

What you need: Nothing

How to play: One person is It, and must loudly count to a predetermined sum, dependent on the number of players and the area they have to hide in. While It counts, the other players find as ingenious hiding places as they can. When the count is finished, It announces 'Ready or not, here I come!' and starts looking for people. The first person found becomes It next round, and the last person found wins.

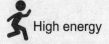 High energy

Hide and Seek Home

An extra element you can add is making the place where the counting happens into a base. When someone is found, if they start running and beat It back to base, they don't become It.

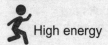 High energy

Soak the Adult

Age: 4 and up

Players: 6 to 12, split into teams, each with as easy-going an adult as is available

What you need: A bucket, a cup and a bottle for each team

How to play: Teams line up behind their bucket of water, while their adults sit with their backs to them, ten or so paces in front, holding bottles on their heads. When the game starts, the first in line in each team fills their cup, runs to their adult and pours the water into the bottle before running back and passing the cup to the next player. The team who fills their bottle first wins. All the adults lose.

 High energy

> **501** *Redress the parent-child getting-wet imbalance with Leaky Lifesaver [245].*

Long-Distance Soaking

A similar set-up but instead of bottles, each adult holds a bucket, and there is a chair about a metre and a half in front of them. Players fill their cups, run to the chair, climb on it and throw as much water as possible into the adults' buckets. Again, extremely easy-going adults are necessary for this game (as are robust chairs).

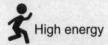 High energy

Dice, Dice, Very Nice

A game that really makes you work hard for some chocolate

Age: 4 and up

Players: 8 and up

What you need: A hat, scarf and gloves, a knife and fork, a dice, a big sharing-sized chocolate bar

How to play: Sit in a circle, with the hat, gloves, cutlery and chocolate bar in the middle. Players take it in turns to throw the dice, and when anyone gets a six, they go into the middle, don the hat and scarf, put the gloves on and start using the knife and fork to unwrap and eat the chocolate. As soon as another player rolls a six, they shout 'Six!' and take over, with the original player ditching everything and going back to their spot. Keep going until the chocolate bar is all gone.

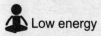 Low energy

> **501** *Fancy a game that involves food, but no deliciousness whatsoever? Pick-up Pasta [23] fits the bill.*

Father Christmas and His Nice Beard

Playing in winter? For a seasonal twist, add a glue stick and a pile of cotton wool balls. The first thing players need to do, before reaching for the hat or scarf, is pop some glue on a cotton wool ball and stick in to their chin. This stays on their chin even when someone else rolls a six. In a long enough game, everyone ends up full of chocolate and looking like Father Christmas.

 Low energy

Card Toss

Age: 4 and up

Players: Any number, split into two even teams

What you need: A deck of cards, a hat or bucket and a hula hoop, coffee table or sheet of newspaper

How to play: Split the cards into red and black – one team gets red and one black. Put the hat or bucket in the middle of the hoop, table or newspaper, and line the teams up 3 or 4 metres away. Alternating between teams, everyone throws one card at a time, trying to get them into the hat, then goes to the back of the line, playing through until all the cards have been thrown. Scores are then calculated – a card in the hat scores 5 points, a card on the brim (if it's that kind of hat) scores 3, and one in the hoop scores 1.

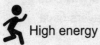 High energy

Under the Cups Memory

A three-dimensional version of the card game (see page 52) that requires a bit more preparation

Age: 5 and up

Players: 4 and up

What you need: As many pairs of small household objects as you can find – anything from two sprouts to two LEGO pieces to two Christmas decorations – and enough identical cups to cover them all

How to play: Arrange the cups, covering the objects, in a grid, not allowing any players to see what has gone under which cup. Players then take it in turns to lift any two cups, looking for pairs, remembering what other players have revealed. Whoever gets the most pairs wins.

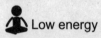 Low energy

501 *Show off more of your memory ability, whether on the road or not, with a game of I Packed My Bag [155].*

Balloon Relay

Not the least wasteful of games, but at least it's really loud!

Age: 5 and up

Players: 4 and up, ideally about 10

What you need: Lots of balloons, a big basket or bin bag per team

How to play: Form equal teams, and divide the balloons up equally into the baskets. Place the baskets 5 metres or so in front of the lined-up teams. At the signal, the first player in each team runs to the basket, takes out a balloon, sits on it until it bursts and runs back. Then the next player goes. The first team to pop all their balloons and return to their starting point wins.

 High energy

Balloon Kneelay

As a slightly quieter alternative, teams start off lined up with a balloon gripped between the front person's knees. They run/waddle to a line 5 metres away and back again, the balloon permanently between their legs and no hands allowed. Then they give the balloon to the next player, and so on. Dropping the balloon incurs a penalty of standing still for two seconds, and a burst balloon means going back to the start.

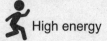 High energy

289

Sardines

Like an alternate-universe Hide And Seek

Age: 5 and up

Players: 6 and up

What you need: Nothing

How to play: One player is sent off to hide while everyone else counts to 50, then goes and looks for them individually. When they find the hiding player, they have to try and join them in the hiding place. The last person to find the amassed players loses and has to be the first to hide next round.

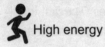 High energy

Simon Says

A lesson in questioning being told what to do

Age: 5 and up

Players: 10 and up

What you need: Nothing

How to play: One adult is in charge, and stands facing everyone else and giving orders, prefaced with 'Simon says'. Things like putting their arms in the air, jumping up and down, or simply 'Simon says do this' (or a different name is thrown in there – 'Euan says sit down') and doing something for players to copy. The thing is, any order that doesn't come 'from Simon' shouldn't be obeyed – if it's just 'Put your arms in the air' or 'Do this', anyone who does it is out. The winner is the last player left in.

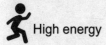 High energy

Rebellious Rule-Breakers

The same set-up, with one adult in charge, but players have to do the opposite of everything they are told. Replace arm with leg and left with right – so, if the adult says 'Wiggle your left arm', anyone who doesn't instead wiggle their right leg is out.

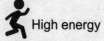 High energy

Musical Chairs

What do you need after a dance? A bit of a sit down. There's just one problem: one chair too few

Age: 5 and up

Players: 10 and up

What you need: Chairs – one fewer than the number of players

How to play: Put some music on, and have everyone dance around the chairs, which can either be in a line in the middle of the room facing in alternate directions, or in a circle facing outwards. When the music stops, everyone has to sit on a chair as quickly as possible – the person who can't get a chair is out, and one chair is removed for the next round. Keep playing until just two extremely careful people are anxiously circling one seat – whoever sits wins.

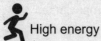 High energy

Musically Marooned

Instead of chairs, spread a sheet or two of newspaper out. If anyone asks, it's a desert island. When the music stops, everyone has to get onto the island. However, every so often, you tear a chunk off it to make it smaller . . .

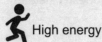 High energy

What's the Time, Mr Wolf?

Lupine temporal explorations resulting in violent consumption

Age: 5 and up

Players: 10 and up

What you need: Nothing

How to play: Play in a large open space. One player is designated Mr Wolf (or, come on, it's the twenty-first century, let's call them something less gendered – Professor Wolf is an extremely cool name), and stands on their own, facing away from everyone else, as far away as they can while remaining within shouting distance. Everyone else stands in a line and calls 'What's the time, [Professor] Wolf?' The wolf calls a time back, and players must walk that many steps forward – six o'clock means six steps and so on. At some point, when the wolf senses someone close, the answer will be 'Dinner time!', at which point the Wolf turns around and tries to tag people (eating them) before they get back to the starting line. Players can try to sneak up and tag Wolf before dinner time, in which case Wolf is bundled off to the zoo and they take over the role.

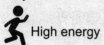 High energy

Traffic Lights

Fast responses are key to success in the sort-of Highway Code

Age: 5 and up

Players: 12 and up – the more the better

What you need: Nothing

How to play: Players need to do whatever the traffic light – the person in charge – tells them to do. Red means lying on the floor being as small as possible. Amber means walking around, and green means running. Shout out the colours – after a few goes to get the hang of it, players who are spotted doing the wrong thing are out. Mix things up by yelling out what everyone is already doing and seeing if anyone panics.

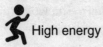
High energy

Traffic Lights in Atlantis

Not a lot of people know this, but traffic lights in Atlantis are really complicated. Blue means stand still while spread as wide as possible, while purple means walking backwards. Very strange place to drive.

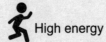
High energy

Thumbs Up

How much can you figure out about someone from the most fleeting of grasps?

Age: 5 and up

Players: 20 or so

What you need: Nothing

How to play: Five or six players are chosen as 'squeezers'. Everyone else lies down with their eyes closed and one thumb up. The squeezers then tiptoe through the group and gently squeeze one – and only one – person's thumb. Players do not open their eyes if their thumb is squeezed. When the squeezers return to the front, everyone opens their eyes and those who had their thumbs squeezed stand up. One by one they guess who squeezed their thumb. The correct culprits are only revealed when everyone has guessed. Correct guessers swap and become squeezers.

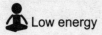 Low energy

Cats and Mice

From Tom and Jerry to Itchy and Scratchy, it's an age-old unresolvable conflict

Age: 5 and up

Players: 20 and up

What you need: Enough 'tails' – a band, ribbon or football sock – for three-quarters of the players

How to play: A quarter of the players are designated 'cats', while the rest of them are 'mice' and tuck a tail into the back of their trousers (the cats, presumably, are Manx). The cats stay in one place while the mice run around until, at the signal, the cats are released. They run around trying to take tails from mice. If a cat gets a tail, they return to the starting point to high-five the adult in charge before rejoining the fray as a mouse. The mouse, having lost its tail, becomes a cat. Yeah, it's not the most biologically accurate of games. Play is theoretically endless, so set a time limit.

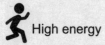 High energy

501 *Fully embody your animal side with Noah's Ark [403].*

Are You Feline Competitive?

Instead of becoming a mouse when they pilfer a tail, cats remain cats until the end, and the number of cats only increases. The game ends with two winners: the last mouse alive, and the cat clutching the most tails.

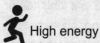 High energy

Telephone

An age-old game of (mis)communication

Age: 5 and up

Players: Any number, the more the merrier

What you need: Nothing

How to play: Everyone stands side by side in a long line or circle. One person whispers a phrase, saying, quote or title into the ear of the person to their left, who in turn whispers it to the next person, and so on. The further it goes, the more likely it is that words will become garbled, the whole message will get confused, and by the time it gets to the last person – who announces it to everyone – you'll often have an unrecognisably different message.

 Low energy

Bugged Lines

Instead of hearing the message and passing it on, players are encouraged to replace one or two words and try to confuse things as much as possible.

 Low energy

Chopsticks and Smarties

Using age-old Chinese eating techniques on sugary snacks

Age: 6 and up, and chopstick experience is a definite advantage

Players: 2 and up

What you need: A bowl, plate and pair of chopsticks for every player, plus plenty of Smarties, M&Ms or similarly round sweets

How to play: Players sit at a table, with a bowl of Smarties, an empty plate and a pair of chopsticks. When the signal is given, move the Smarties one at a time from bowl to plate using the chopsticks. The winner is either the first to finish or the person to do the most within a time limit. Alternatively, just eat the Smarties with the chopsticks – it's fun and delicious!

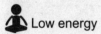 Low energy

Chopstick Run

Can you go from one room to another precariously carrying a Smartie in some chopsticks? Adding a distance or obstacles between the bowl and plate makes for an infuriatingly difficult (yet similarly deliciously rewarding) challenge.

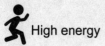 High energy

Peg Pick-up

Stretching little hands to their limits

Age: 6 and up

Players: 2 to 4

What you need: Clothes pegs

How to play: Six clothes pegs are placed in front of each player. At the signal, everyone picks up the pegs one at a time with one hand only, raising their hand above their head in between each one. If any drop, they must start again. The winner is the first to pick up all of the pegs.

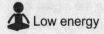 Low energy

Peg Relay

Form teams of four or so. Position the pegs at 3-metre intervals in front of each team. At the signal, the first player from each team has to run the course, picking up a peg at each stop, all in one hand, then run back and hand them to the next player, who takes them in one hand and runs the course placing one peg at each interval. If any pegs are dropped, that player has to start their run again. The first team to 'complete' the course wins.

 High energy

Balloon Burst

Extremely loud, very messy and a lot of fun

Age: 6 and up

Players: 2 and up – ideally about 8

What you need: Lots of balloons, pen and paper

How to play: Blow up loads and loads of balloons, hiding a small piece of paper in one of them (a kitchen funnel can help if struggling to get it in) with a secret password on it. Players split into two teams and send one person at a time to go to town on the balloons, one pop at a time. The first person to come and tell the password to the person in charge wins for their team.

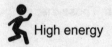 High energy

Zip Bong

A deeply silly quest to not laugh

Age: 6 and up

Players: 3 and up – the more the merrier really

What you need: Nothing

How to play: Sit in a circle, with players curling their top lips inwards as best they can to reveal lots of teeth and ensure everyone looks ridiculous. One person begins, and 'passes' the word 'zip' to the person to their left, who in turn passes it on, and so on, building up speed. If anyone chooses to say 'bong' instead, the direction is reversed. Try frantically to stay in as the game speeds up, without either missing your turn, relaxing your mouth or starting to laugh. Those that do are eliminated.

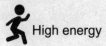 High energy

Zip Bong X-Ray

Adding extra elements like 'X-ray' (continuing in the same direction but skipping one person) or 'lob' (accompanied by pointing to someone else in the circle), all while keeping your lips over your teeth, can make proceedings even sillier.

 High energy

Pretzel

A DIY version of a limb-twisting challenge

Age: 6 and up

Players: 3 and up

What you need: Construction paper in six different colours, tape, two different dice

How to play: Tape the paper to the floor in a neat grid, one colour to each row. Assign one dice to colours – one for red, two for blue, etc – and the other to limbs – a one is the left arm and so on, with five and six just meaning 'roll again'. Throwing the two dice presents you with combinations like 'left foot orange', at which point players have to move their left foot to an orange sheet. The more limbs get involved, the more entwined the players become. When someone falls or can't manage to reach the right colour, they are out. Last player, er, 'standing' (?) wins.

 High energy

> **501** *While you've got the paper and tape out, give Green's on Fire [330] a go.*

Limb Chaos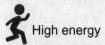

As above, but even more chaotic: sacrifice the order of the neat grid in favour of a messy array of different coloured paper, as overlapping or annoying to access as you wish.

 High energy

You Limb Sum, You Lose Some

Instead of using coloured paper, normal paper is used, with a one-digit number written on each sheet. Each player starts with their left hand on a different number – say, seven, five and three with three players – then has to put their right hand on whatever would need to be added to make ten. Then they get a different number each for their left foot, and another randomly selected total to make with their right, and so on.

 High energy

Sweetie in a Haystack

Either a waste of pasta or a totally awesome use of pasta

Age: 6 and up

Players: 3 and up

What you need: A large amount of cooked, cooled spaghetti (with a bit of olive oil in to stop it clumping together), some small sweets like Smarties, plates, cups

How to play: Each player has a big plate of spaghetti placed in front of them, each with five sweets mixed in. They also have a cup. On the signal, keeping their hands behind their backs, they have to try to get to the sweets, pick them up with their mouths and deposit them in the cup. Their hands must stay behind their backs at all times. The first person to get a cup with five sweets in wins.

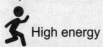 High energy

305 *A Smartie at a party? For more rhyming fun, try Rhyming Nicknames [167].*

Stacked Sweetie Selection

Mix in two colours of sweets, in larger quantities – say, half red, half blue. Players have 1 minute to fill their cup with as many red sweets as possible. Any blue one that gets in doesn't just not count, it also comes off their total.

 High energy

Dangling Doughnuts

Deliciously competitive, competitively delicious

Age: 6 and up

Players: 3 and up

What you need: A ring doughnut per player, string

How to play: String up a doughnut per player, dangling at around head height, from tree branches or railings. Players step up to their doughnuts with their hands behind their backs and, when the signal is given, everyone starts eating, hands remaining behind backs at all times. The first person to finish their doughnut jumps up and down with their hands in the air so everyone knows they've won.

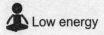 Low energy

Dangling Deliciousness

There are plenty of foods that can be dangled that are slightly healthier than doughnuts. Using skewers to poke holes through veg and and threading knotted string through can lead to a much more vitamin-filled variation of this game.

 Low energy

Toe Tap

A no-holds-barred battle, mandible à mandible

Age: 6 and up

Players: Any even number

What you need: Nothing

How to play: Play in twos, ideally with a partner of similar size. Players face each other, holding onto one another's shoulders. The aim is to tap your opponent's toe with yours, while they try to both prevent that and tap yours instead. One point is scored for each tap, but it's tapping only – no stamping or kicking. Stamping or kicking awards your rival 3 points. First to 10 wins.

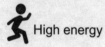 High energy

Chopscotch

A hopping relay involving a bit of nimbleness

Age: 6 and up

Players: Any even number

What you need: Ten chopsticks per team

How to play: Form teams of two or more. Lay the chopsticks out on the floor in front of each team at intervals of 25cm or so. At the signal, the first player from each team hops over every stick to the end, picks up the last stick (while still hopping) and hops back. The second player then does the same, and so on until one team has all their sticks. If anyone touches a stick with their foot or puts their second foot down, they start that run again.

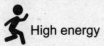 High energy

Water Balloon Piñata

A Mexican-influenced game where the real winner is gravity

Age: 6 and up

Players: Any number

What you need: Water balloons, string, wooden spoons, dice

How to play: Fill a water balloon and hang it, using the string, from a tree branch or something similar (and outdoors, of course), so it is above head height for the children playing. Players take it in turns to roll a dice. They then have to stand under the water balloon and hit it with a wooden spoon, the same amount of times as spots were shown on the dice. If their hit is judged to not be hard enough, they have to do it again.

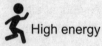 High energy

Paired Piñata

Form teams of two. One sits under the piñata, and has 10 seconds to name five things in a category given to them by their partner. If they can't do it, or get any wrong, their partner hits the piñata as many times as the points they didn't get.

 High energy

Pin the Tail on the Donkey

The age-old combination of blindfolds, farming and DIY appendage reattachment surgery

Age: 6 and up

Players: 4 to 6

What you need: Paper, pens, preparation, a blindfold

How to play: Print out, or draw, a large donkey devoid of a tail, affix it to a vertical surface, and make a tail from a strip of paper (depending on surfaces, it might be more 'tape the tail to the donkey' in reality). Players take it in turns to be blindfolded, approach the donkey and put the tail where they think it should go. An X is then drawn where they put it, along with their name, and the tail and blindfold are passed to the next player. The closest to the correct spot wins.

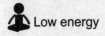 Low energy

Pin the Donkey on the Donkey

Why limit oneself to a tail? Divide the donkey into as many parts as there are players – for example, with six players, you could have a torso on the wall, four players with legs, one with a head and one with a tail.

 Low energy

Spider's Web

Part darts, part nature documentary, all blindfolded guesswork

Age: 6 and up

Players: 4 and up

What you need: A whiteboard, easel or large piece of paper and tape, three cut-out cardboard spiders with double-sided tape on, a blindfold

How to play: Before playing, draw a spider web with three tiers of scores coming out from the centre – the further away from the centre, the higher the score. Centre tier scores 1, next scores 3, outermost tier scores 5, but missing the outermost tier scores 0. Blindfolded, spun-around players are given three spiders and have to first find the web and then stick them on. If multiple players get the same high score, they compete again until one person reigns supreme as Arachnid Ruler.

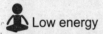 Low energy

501 *More eight-legged fun: Octopus Alert [232].*

I, Fly

The same set-up, but have three spiders drawn on the web from the get-go, and make three paper flies with tape on. Players must, blindfolded, place their flies as safely as possible on the web while trying to score as highly as possible. Any fly touching a spider scores nothing.

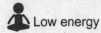 Low energy

Box of Delights

Can you see with your hands?

Age: 6 and up

Players: 4 and up

What you need: A cardboard box, a cloth or tea towel, pens and paper, assorted household items.

How to play: Gather a bunch of items together beforehand with different shapes and textures (say, a whisk, a teddy bear, a satsuma, some sandpaper and a bar of soap) and put them in the box. Cover the top of it with the cloth so nobody can see its contents. Players take it in turns to reach in without looking and feel around for 10 seconds. They can then write down everything they think is in there. When everyone has had a go, reveal the contents and whoever got the most right wins.

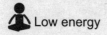 Low energy

Socks of Delight

Alternatively, place various objects in the toes of socks and challenge players to identify the contents of all ten (or however many) socks just by feel. Most points wins.

 Low energy

Sweet, Sweet Memories

A delicious variation on a classic memory game

Age: 6 and up

Players: 4 and up

What you need: A big packet of identical wrapped sweets (at least 16) – anything from fun-size Mars bars to one flavour of Starburst, stickers, a pen

How to play: Put numbered stickers on the undersides of the sweets – two of each number – and arrange them in a grid. Players take it in turns to turn two over, looking for matching pairs. If you find a pair, you keep it. Whoever has the most at the end of the game, minus any they've eaten out of impatience, wins.

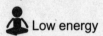 Low energy

Flour Power

A messy, messy game best suited to outdoor play

Age: 6 and up

Players: 4 and up

What you need: A bowl, a knife (ideally a plastic one or butter knife), a bag of flour, a counter or LEGO figure, a plate

How to play: Pack the bowl tightly with flour and invert it onto the plate – lifting it off should leave you with a sandcastle-like structure. Carefully place the counter or figure on top of it. Players take it in turns to use the knife to cut a slice out of the flour cake, trying not to disturb the counter. Do you cut a tiny sliver, or do you cut as large a one as you dare, to try and sabotage the next player? Whoever sends the counter falling has to retrieve it using their teeth and is likely to end up extremely floury.

 Low energy

Mouths and Marbles

Using puff-power

Age: 6 and up

Players: 4 and up

What you need: Straws, marbles, a bowl, a wide-necked bottle

How to play: Players take it in turns to see how many marbles they can transport from the bowl to the bottle in 60 seconds by sucking them with a straw – no hands are allowed at all.

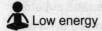 Low energy

Many-Mouthed Marbles

Form teams and pass the marbles from the front to the back, handing them over from straw to straw. It's really hard! Some will drop! Start off as many as possible to compensate!

 High energy

Kim's Game

This game features in Kim *by Rudyard Kipling, which is proof that this book is really highbrow*

Age: 6 and up

Players: 4 and up

What you need: A tray of various household objects, a cloth or towel, a timer, pencils and paper for everyone

How to play: In full view of all players, proudly unveil a tray containing a selection of 15 to 20 objects (fewer if playing with younger kids). Give everyone 30 seconds to soak it in before covering them up again, at which point everyone can lift their pens and paper and have 2½ minutes to write down everything they remember. One point per item remembered, most points wins, bish bash bosh.

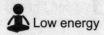 Low energy

What's Missing?

Another way of playing: show everyone the tray, then leave the room and re-enter a few seconds later having removed one item. The first person to raise their hand and name it wins.

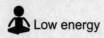 Low energy

Real-World Spot the Difference

The printed world's favourite puzzle with an added third dimension running along in the background

Age: 6 and up

Players: 4 and up

What you need: A selection of household objects

How to play: Position a selection of objects on a table or in a corner. Tell everyone that at some point during the day, when nobody is looking, you will make a difference to it. Then, at a point when everyone is otherwise occupied, quickly change the amount of liquid in that jug, reorder that line of sweets, swap those two pens around, or whatever. The first person to spot the difference and report it to the person in charge gets some kind of bonus prize.

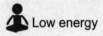 Low energy

Human Mirror

An opportunity for self-reflection

Age: 6 and up

Players: 4 and up

What you need: Nothing

How to play: Players form pairs and face one another. Everyone facing one direction is a person, while everyone facing the other direction is their reflection. The person in charge shouts out commands that can be fairly freely interpreted – anything from 'Dance!' to 'Do science!' The 'people' interpret it however they want, and their reflections follow suit. Every minute, or at completely arbitrary periods, the person in charge can shout 'Switch!', and all of a sudden the roles of person and reflection are reversed. Keep going until everything descends into complete nonsense.

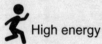 High energy

Egg and Spoon Race

A protein-heavy competition

Age: 6 and up

Players: 4 and up

What you need: One egg and one spoon per competitor (or team)

How to play: Competitors line up at the starting line, each holding a spoon with an egg balanced on it. At the signal, they try and race towards the finish line without the egg falling off – if the egg breaks, they are disqualified. Lemons can be substituted as a less breakable alternative.

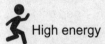 High energy

> **501** *Put your spoons to further use with a game of Connect-the-Kids [372].*

Egg on Your Face

To make things extra hard, try running a race with an egg balanced on a spoon, and the spoon gripped in your mouth.

 High energy

Three-Legged Race

Speed, mutual coordination and a determination not to fall over

Age: 6 and up

Players: 4 and up

What you need: Bandages, or as near to bandages as you have to hand

How to play: Form teams of two, and stand side by side, arms around each other's shoulders. A grown-up then ties together the two legs in the middle, forming a two-headed person with three legs. Teams line up and, on a signal, run to a designated spot while trying not to go flying.

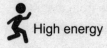 High energy

Charades

Always popular at Christmas, combining pop-culture knowledge and excruciating acting. Just be sure to write appropriate clues for the crowd

Age: 6 and up

Players: 6 and up

What you need: Pens, paper, a timer

How to play: Either prepare cards beforehand or have everyone spend some time writing things (films, books, songs and TV shows) on scraps of paper for other people to enact. Depending on how many players there are, teams or individual play might make more sense. Players take it in turns to stand in front of everyone, take a clue from the bag and wordlessly communicate it (if playing in teams, you use clues written by the other team and try to communicate them to your own). Use your hands to show the number of words and the type of title (making a screen with your fingers for a TV show, miming a video camera for a film, pretending to read for a book and doing an operatic pose for a song), and then do whatever you need to in 30 seconds to get the idea across and score the point.

 Low energy

Express Charades

Instead of trying to perform one clue with a 30-second limit, players have 1 minute to do as many as they can.

 Low energy

Impression Charades

Much like normal charades, but instead of titles, the clues are a mixture of famous people and animal species, and players must use the best of their acting ability to get them across to their teammates.

 Low energy

Stony Silence

An astonishingly quiet rowdy game

Age: 6 and up

Players: 6 and up

What you need: A ball

How to play: Players throw the ball from one to another, absolutely silently. Anyone who speaks is out. Anyone who drops the ball is out. Anyone who throws the ball so dreadfully that nobody could even dream of catching it is out. Play until only one person is left, and then shout at them.

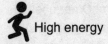 High energy

Pass the Sample

A disgusting game of textures and unseen vileness

Age: 6 and up

Players: 6 and up

What you need: At least one cardboard box with a hole cut in the side so people can reach in to feel the contents but not see in, pens and paper, various foods

How to play: Pass a box around telling players it contains human teeth and giving them turns reaching in and feeling the contents. Can they identify what it actually contains from touch alone, and write it down? It's sweetcorn! Other ones to try: eyeballs (peeled grapes), human skin (cut-up balloons), mouse poos (uncooked rice), worms (cooked spaghetti), cats' hearts (tinned tomatoes), removed warts (dried peas), and anything disgusting that springs to mind. Whoever identifies the most wins.

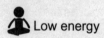 Low energy

Human Dartboard

Not as grisly as it sounds

Age: 6 and up

Players: 6 and up

What you need: Chalk, a blindfold

How to play: Draw three big concentric circles on the ground – the middle one about 2 metres in diameter, the next 3, the next 4. Now draw lines across the whole thing splitting it into eight segments (so, 24 'cells'). Mark the segments one to eight in a random order. Split the players into two teams. One at a time, players stand in the centre blindfolded and are spun around three times. They then have to walk forward a few steps and shout 'Here!', at which point their team gets the amount of points of the segment they're in multiplied by which ring they're in – one for the innermost circle, two for the next and three for the outermost. If they go beyond the outermost circle, they score nothing. The first team to 100 wins.

 Low energy

> **501** *Darts skills can be put to the test with an arachnid twist in Spider's Web [313].*

Human Dartboard Doubles

Play in pairs – one player in the middle, one to the side.
The player in the middle holds four beanbags, stones or
toys – anything that isn't going to roll away. After they are
spun around, they have 10 seconds to walk around and
put their bags down, as directed by their non-blindfolded
teammate outside. Points are scored by where the bags
are placed – however, if multiple bags are put down in
the same cell, only one of them counts.

 Low energy

Sharks and Desert Islands

The last thing anyone needs on a desert island is a shark

Age: 6 and up

Players: 6 and up

What you need: Chalk, a source of music, a bucket

How to play: Draw a few desert islands on the ground, with as much or as little detail as you like (they're not going to last long). Play some music as the players 'swim around' – when the music stops they need to jump onto an island. The last person to get to an island gets eaten by a shark, and then *becomes* a shark. The shark's job is to get in people's way as they head towards an island, and the last person to make it to land each time becomes another shark. Every so often, there might be a storm, which involves pouring a bucket of water over one of the islands to get rid of the chalk and create more distance. The last surviving human wins.

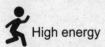 High energy

Green's on Fire

An arbitrary game of stepping stones and sudden disasters

Age: 6 and up

Players: 6 and up

What you need: A packet of coloured construction paper, tape

How to play: Tape the pieces of paper to the ground in a big circle so the colours are all mixed up. Players step from one to another like stepping stones. Every so often, the person in charge shouts 'Stop!', and the players must all stop on one piece. One colour of paper is then announced as being on fire, and all the players standing on that colour are out (depending on how many colours of paper there are, the person in charge can use a dice, or a flicked-through pad of the remaining colours, or various other impartial methods to select what colour combusts). After each fire, every colour is fine again. Keep going until only one player remains.

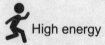 High energy

501 *Fires need putting out! Could the answer be . . . Cup Firefighters [373]?*

Ibble Dibble

A deeply silly game best played by people too young to have facial hair

Age: 6 and up

Players: 6 and up

What you need: Stickers, plus pennies or counters for lives

How to play: Everyone sits in a circle and is given a number, as well as three lives. The first player says 'I, ibble dibble number one, with no ibble dibbles, ibble dibble you, ibble dibble number [any player of their choice, who they point to], with no ibble dibbles, ibble dibble.' The player pointed to then does the same, pointing at someone else. If anyone gets it wrong, they throw a life into the middle of the circle and have a sticker stuck to their face. They then describe themselves as having 'one ibble dibble', and so on. Keep going until only one player remains alive. What a silly game.

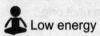 Low energy

Breakaway

Suspense, secrets and sprinting

Age: 6 and up

Players: 6 and up

What you need: One playing card per player, one of which is unique – all reds and one black, for instance

How to play: Everyone draws a card, keeping it secret. The black card is the sprint card, and whoever has that is in a pretty great position. Everyone starts lined up side by side, aiming to get over a line at the other side of the playing area before as many of their opponents as possible. The thing is, they can only walk. At any given point, though, the player who has the sprint card can start running. Once they're running, everyone else can run as well. The last player to cross the line is out. The cards are gathered up, one red one is discarded, and the whole thing begins again. The slowest player to cross the line is eliminated each time until one person is crowned champion.

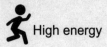 High energy

Tennis Neck

Not connected to tennis elbow, just a sensible name for a game involving necks and tennis balls

Age: 6 and up

Players: 8 and up

What you need: One tennis ball per team

How to play: Line up in teams of four or more. The first person in each team starts off with a tennis ball gripped between their chin and chest. On the signal, they have to pass it back through every member of the team with everyone's hands remaining behind their back.

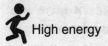 High energy

Bing Bang Whoops

A space-age game of invisible laser weaponry

Age: 6 and up

Players: 8 and up

What you need: Pennies or counters for lives

How to play: Players sit in a circle, each with three lives. One player starts off with an imaginary ray gun. They have the choice of saying 'Bing' and pointing at someone (which passes the ray gun to them) or 'Bang' (which fires it at them). If the gun is fired, the people sitting on either side of the person it's fired at shout 'Whoops!' and put their hands in the air. Then the person who was fired at continues. Anyone who doesn't do the 'Whoops!', or does it when they shouldn't, loses a life and throws it into the middle of the circle. If at any point the player with the ray gun points it at the ceiling and shouts 'Bang!', everyone in the whole circle has to shout 'Whoops!' and raise their arms. When players lose all their lives they are eliminated and leave the circle.

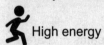 High energy

Make Me a Mummy

As absolutely not played in Ancient Egypt

Age: 6 and up

Players: 8 and up

What you need: Several toilet rolls, a timer

How to play: Form teams of four. Each team chooses one person to be the Mummy, and has 2 minutes to wrap them in toilet paper to transform them into the spitting image of a long-dead pharaoh. They should be as hidden as possible, obscured under layers of the stuff. When the time limit is up, teams are awarded points – they start with 10 and lose 1 for every actual body part the judge/timekeeper can see.

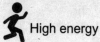 High energy

Mummy Race

Making sure to wrap each leg separately, teams prepare a Mummy, and the Mummies are pitted against one another in a straightforward race. Well, as straightforward as not really being able to see and being covered in loo roll is.

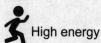 High energy

What a Cairo-on

Look, you can't expect a pharaoh to do their own running. They're far too important for that. Teams bind their Mummy in toilet roll, then race one another, carrying their Mummy between the three of them. Some go for a surfboard grip, some for the sack-of-potatoes style, all need to be careful not to drop their friend – still, in the event of bleeding, toilet paper is very absorbent.

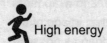 High energy

Zombie Tag

An indoor tagging game of terrifyingly close quarters

Age: 6 and up

Players: 8 and up

What you need: Nothing

How to play: Best played in quite a confined space. One player is It, an incredibly infectious zombie. Zombies can't run, of course, so they just move about within a fairly small room, arms out in front of them, moaning, trying to corner people and tag them. Tagged people become zombies as well. The last non-zombie wins.

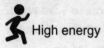 High energy

Snowflake Race

How fast can you run with a snowflake on your head?

Age: 6 and up

Players: 8 and up

What you need: Paper, scissors, as many obstacles as possible

How to play: Start by everyone making a paper snowflake – fold a sheet of paper into quarters and cut bits away so that when it's unfolded you have a lovely-looking, rotationally symmetrical work of art. Form teams of four. Players have to balance the snowflake on their heads and keep their hands in their pockets while navigating a slalom-like course – weaving in and out of obstacles. If the snowflake falls off, they have to sit down cross-legged on the floor to pick it up, losing valuable time, before getting up, replacing it on their head and continuing. The first team with all members to complete the course wins.

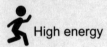 High energy

Cross-Country Leapfrog

It's not the most dignified way to travel, but it works

Age: 6 and up

Players: 8 and up

What you need: Nothing

How to play: Form teams of four or so. Each team stands in a line about a metre apart behind a start line, and a finish line/point is decided upon. On the signal, everyone but the back player bends over, and the back player leapfrogs over all of them in turn before joining the front of their team's line. The player who is now at the back does the same thing. Keep going, with the whole team gradually moving forward towards the finish line. The first team to reach it wins, but anyone having to take a step between leapfrogs (due to players trying to inch forward and steal a bit of distance) has to rejoin their line from the back.

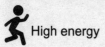 High energy

Hoop Relay

Accuracy is more essential than speed in this race

Age: 6 and up

Players: 8 and up, in teams of four

What you need: Three hula hoops (or rope laid in a circle, or circles of 1-metre diameter drawn in chalk) and a beanbag (or anything else that is throwable but doesn't bounce) per team

How to play: Place the hoops at regular intervals in front of each lined-up team. Players have to throw the beanbag into the first hoop before they can run to it – if they miss, they have to retrieve the beanbag and throw again. Once they get the bag in the hoop, they run to the hoop and throw the beanbag into the next one. When they get to the last hoop, they run back and hand the bag over to the next player. The first team to complete the course wins.

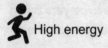 High energy

Commando Race

Add as many weird, wacky and wonderful stages as you like – players can crawl under tarpaulins like they're on an army assault course, or weave in and out of cones like Olympic skiers, or jump from haybale to haybale. Use whatever is to hand to create a multi-stage course requiring different skills.

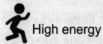 High energy

Human Boules

Who needs balls when you have people?

Age: 6 and up

Players: 10 and up

What you need: Chalk and a surface you can draw on, as many blindfolds as possible

How to play: Split into teams of four or so. Draw three large concentric circles on the ground – the centre one about half a metre in diameter, the next 1 metre, the third 2 metres. The centre circle scores 20 points, the next one 10, the outermost one 5. Now draw a line about 1 metre away from the outside circle, and another one 4 metres behind that. Teams line up next to one another behind this line and take it in turns to send a blindfolded member up to the circles, aiming to get them into the centre circle for the most points, shouting directions at them. Once they hit the 1-metre line, their teams can't direct them anymore. If two human boules collide, the one who has been hit has to take a step away from the boule that hit them, who has to stop. Think tactically about the order you go in, as blindfolded players can't do much directing. When it is the turn of the last player in each team, the other players can remove their blindfolds and all direct them at once. The winner is the team with most points when everyone has been 'thrown'.

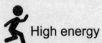 High energy

501 *If you enjoy becoming a boule, why not try becoming a dart on a Human Dartboard [327]?*

Blind Man's Buff

Experience the world hands first

Age: 6 and up

Players: 10 and up

What you need: A blindfold

How to play: Play in a clearly defined space – one room, for instance. One player is It, and is blindfolded and (optionally) spun around a few times. They then have to try and tag other players, who are out when tagged. The last player standing wins, and gets to be It next time.

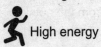 High energy

Buff Mush

Add a rule where the players are only out if It is capable of identifying the person they have captured by feeling their face.

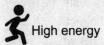 High energy

Face Feel

Age: 6 and up

Players: 10 and up

What you need: A blindfold, a timer

How to play: One player is blindfolded and everyone else forms a queue in front of them. How many people can the blindfolded player identify by feeling their faces in 1 minute? Really mess with their heads by having people who have already been felt rejoin the queue.

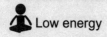 Low energy

Duck Duck Goose

A game where fowl play is the only way

Age: 6 and up

Players: 10 and up

What you need: Nothing

How to play: Everyone sits on the floor in a circle apart from one person, who is It. It walks around the outside of the circle, tapping everyone on the head in turn and saying 'Duck, duck, duck, duck . . .' At one point, rather than duck, they say 'Goose!' They and the goose then have to run around the circle – It on the outside and the goose on the inside – and It must try to take the goose's place in the circle.

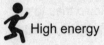 High energy

You You Me

Instead of ducks and geese, It walks around tapping everyone on the head and saying their names. At one point they tap someone's head and say their own name instead, at which point chaos ensues.

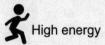 High energy

Seat Scramble

Like musical chairs, with music replaced by insight

Age: 6 and up

Players: 10 and up

What you need: Chairs – one fewer than the number of players

How to play: Arrange the seats in a circle facing inwards, with one player in the middle of the circle and all the seats occupied. The player in the middle says 'Change seats if you . . .' and a category of their choosing. If you're a boy, if your age is an even number, if you were born in the summer, if you're wearing jeans – anything. Anyone who it applies to has to change seats, and the player in the middle tries to get one in the scramble. Whoever is left over is now in the middle. If anyone is stuck in the middle for more than three goes, they are out, one chair is removed and someone else starts in the middle.

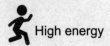 High energy

Musical Hats

The worlds of music and millinery collide

Age: 6 and up

Players: 10 and up

What you need: Hats – one fewer than the number of players

How to play: Pile the hats in the centre of the room, put music on and have everyone dance around. When the music stops, the last person to put on a hat is out and one hat is removed. If playing, it's worth thinking tactically about what hat to go for – if there's one particularly cool one, everybody's going to go for it, so you might be as well swooping in to don the really rubbish-looking one . . .

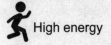 High energy

Musical Statues

From dynamic dancing to stock still in a heartbeat

Age: 6 and up

Players: 10 and up

What you need: Nothing

How to play: Put some music on and get everyone dancing.
When the music stops abruptly, they have to stay as still as
possible, even if they're in a silly position from dancing. The
last person to stop is out. The more upbeat and intense the
music, the harder it is to suddenly halt . . .

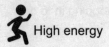 High energy

Musical Bumps

Rather than standing perfectly still when the music stops,
partygoers have to hit the deck – the last person to go
from dancing to sitting/lying down is out.

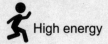 High energy

Frozen Friends

Rather than waiting for the music to stop and freezing then, one person is secretly told that they are the freezing friend. At any given point, they freeze completely still, and the last person to spot them and also freeze is out.

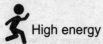 High energy

Musical Potato

Keep that spud moving or risk elimination!

Age: 6 and up

Players: 10 and up

What you need: A tennis ball or beanbag

How to play: Throw a ball from person to person while music plays – ideally dancing around as well. Whoever is holding it when the music stops is out, but players are also eliminated if they hold on to the ball for too long or seem like they deliberately miss a catch or throw it towards nobody.

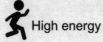 High energy

Musical Dice Unlucky Explosion

An entirely arbitrary game . . . of death!

Age: 6 and up

Players: 10 and up

What you need: A dice, six hula hoops or sheets of newspaper numbered 1 to 6

How to play: As the music plays, everyone dances about or runs around. When it stops, everyone has to get to one of the numbered areas. While there are more than six players, no area can be left unoccupied, so people slower to scramble to their number of choice might find themselves relegated to another one. The person in charge of the music then rolls a dice. Whatever number they roll immediately explodes (overacting is very much encouraged) and everyone in that area is out. Play then continues. When there are six players or fewer, only one person can be in each area. The winner is the final survivor.

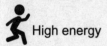 High energy

Shoe Shuttle

A game of quick reflexes and quality footwear

Age: 6 and up

Players: 10 and up

What you need: A bunch of shoes

How to play: Players are split into two teams, and each player on each team is given a number. Teams line up on opposite sides of the playing area. The person in charge throws a shoe into the middle of the playing area and shouts a number, and the child from each team with that number runs out and tries to get the shoe before their opponent does. Play until the grown-up in charge is out of shoes. Teams score 1 point per shoe, with a bonus point for every complete pair.

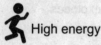 High energy

Territorial Balloons

A frantic battle to clear your area

Age: 6 and up

Players: 10 and up

What you need: Lots and lots of balloons or scrunched-up bits of paper in two colours, a timer

How to play: Use tape or string to make a line down the middle of the space (or use a boundary that is already there) and split into two teams. Divide the balloons so each team has one colour. You have 2 minutes to get all your balloons over the line into the other team's area, while trying to keep theirs out of yours. The timer needs to be extremely strict, with the last 5 seconds counted down loudly by the timekeeper. The balloons are then totalled up, and whichever team managed to keep their area as balloon-free as possible wins.

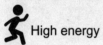 High energy

Pass the Sausage

A team game of dextrous knees

Age: 6 and up

Players: 10 and up

What you need: Long balloons

How to play: Split into teams of four or five. The person at the front grips the balloon between their knees and, when everyone is told to go, turns around and passes it to the next person, with no hands being used at any point. Keep the balloon going to the person at the back, who has to turn around three times with the balloon between their knees, then send it back to the person at the front. If anyone drops the balloon, they have to pick it up without using their hands. It's worth having a few spares knocking around in case of poppage – teams who pop their balloon start again from the front.

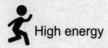 High energy

Pass the Cards

The player at the front begins with a card that they keep to their lips by sucking. It has to be passed, hands-free, mouth-to-mouth, to the back. Very much not a game for everyone.

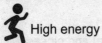 High energy

Toilet Paper Toes

Everyone removes their shoes and socks, and passes cardboard tubes taken from the inside of toilet rolls or kitchen rolls from the front of the line to the back using their big toes. A word of warning: this game can be disgustingly smelly.

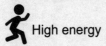 High energy

Fish and Chips

A game of disguised voices and audible obfuscation

Age: 6 and up

Players: 10 and up

What you need: Nothing

How to play: One player comes to the front and closes their eyes. The person in charge then points to another player, who can move to another spot if they wish before saying 'Fish and chips' in as different a voice to their own as they can. The player at the front has two chances to guess who it is. If they are right on their first guess, they win 2 points. If they are right on their second guess, they win 1. If they are wrong, the person who spoke takes their place at the front. The player with the most points after five minutes of play wins.

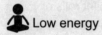 Low energy

Catch the Dragon's Tail

A traditional Chinese game for loads of people

Age: 6 and up

Players: 10 and up

What you need: Nothing

How to play: All the players form a line, with their hands on the shoulders of the player in front. The person at the front is the dragon's head, while the person at the back is the dragon's tail. The dragon's head tries to twist the whole dragon around in order to tag the tail, while the players in the dragon's body do their best to prevent it happening. When the tail is tagged, they move to the front and become the dragon's new head.

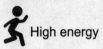 High energy

Kicking Rounders

A football-based game you don't need to be good at football for

Age: 6 and up

Players: 10 and up

What you need: A football, four things to work as bases

How to play: Play with normal rounders rules, but instead of bowling to a batter, the 'batter' is fed the ball to kick. However, it has to stay at ground level – no hoofing it over everyone's heads. Fielders can throw, kick or do whatever is necessary to try and stump 'batters' out.

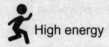 High energy

Silent Ball

Silence is golden, and so are medals

Age: 6 and up

Players: 10 and up

What you need: Any kind of ball

How to play: Players stand in a circle and throw a ball back and forth without speaking. If someone misses, they are out and sit on the floor. However, people who are out are allowed to speak as much as they want, and can distract other players to their heart's content. Keep playing until there is one winner.

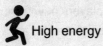 High energy

European Rules Silent Ball

Two extra rules to keep things interesting: first, if anyone does a really bad uncatchable throw and more than three other players point at them, they're out instead of the player who failed to catch it. Secondly, seated players can re-enter the game by catching the ball.

 High energy

Make Me a Masterpiece

A two-person creative process where nobody knows who they're working with

Age: 6 and up

Players: 10 and up

What you need: Pens and paper

How to play: Every player is given a piece of paper and a pen, and given 1 minute to scribble on it. The papers are then gathered up, shuffled and redistributed, and players now have 2 minutes to make the scribble they have been given into as good a piece of artwork as they can. It's more about seeing what people end up with than actual competition, a celebration of how working together can turn nonsense into gold.

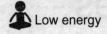 Low energy

Make Me an Exhibition

After the first player has scribbled, a theme is then announced for everyone's pictures, so the second player has to work with what they've got and make it make sense as part of, say, an exhibition of 'adventure', 'body parts' or 'foods of the world'.

 Low energy

Under the Sea

All the magic of the bottom of the ocean from the comfort of somewhere with oxygen

Age: 6 and up

Players: 10 and up

What you need: Nothing

How to play: Form teams of two. Each team is assigned the name of a sea creature and lies down, feet apart but touching one another's, in a line. When everyone is lying down it should almost look like a ladder made of legs, with torsos hanging off the side. The person in charge slowly makes up a story set at the bottom of the ocean, and every time a creature one of the pairs is named after is mentioned, they have to jump up and run over everyone else's legs and back to their spot, going around when they get to the end. However, because this is all taking place at the bottom of the sea, they have to do swimming motions with their hands the whole way. As the story gets more complicated, multiple teams can be called at once. Rather than there being a winner, the game ends when it descends into unplayable chaos.

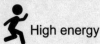 High energy

Whoozit

How well can everyone work together to keep one player in the dark?

Age: 6 and up

Players: 12 and up

What you need: Nothing

How to play: Everyone stands in a circle around one player, the detective, who closes their eyes while one person in the circle is (silently) designated the Whoozit. The Whoozit starts to do some sort of easily-copyable rhythmic action – patting themselves on the stomach, rocking from side to side, jumping up and down, etc, and everyone else copies them. When the detective opens their eyes, they have to try to figure out who the Whoozit is, but every 20 seconds, the Whoozit has to change what they're doing and everyone else has to catch up. Can the detective figure out who everyone is copying?

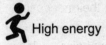 High energy

Animal Acrostic

Animals on animals on animals

Age: 6 and up

Players: 12 and up

What you need: Pens and paper

How to play: Split into teams of four or five. Each team is assigned an animal, each with the same number of letters but no repeated letters – say, donkey, lizard, wombat and falcon. This is written down the side of each team's sheet. Everyone then has 3 minutes to come up with as many animals beginning with each letter of their team animal as possible. The team with the most (and there might be some arguments about whether, say, a dinosaur species counts as an animal) wins.

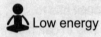 Low energy

Polos and Straws

Use teamwork and precision to inefficiently transport confectionery

Age: 6 and up

Players: 12 and up

What you need: One narrow straw per person, bowls, Polos or any other sweets with holes in

How to play: Every player has a straw. Teams of six or so line up. The player at the front has a bowl with Polos in it, and the player at the back has an empty bowl. At the signal, teams begin transporting one Polo at a time using only straws gripped between their teeth, passing them from straw to straw carefully. The first to transfer ten mints, or the team to have the most after a certain time limit, wins. A dropped Polo remains on the ground.

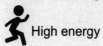 High energy

Mint Toothpicks

Make the game even harder by replacing the straws with toothpicks (with the ends snapped off to avoid skewering of faces).

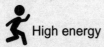 High energy

Team Slalom

Weave in and out of teammates to make your way to the front

Age: 6 and up

Players: 12 and up

What you need: Nothing

How to play: Form teams of six or so and stand in a line, 2 metres apart. On the signal, the person at the back runs in and out of their team until they are at the front, then shouts 'Go!', at which point the player who is now at the back does the same. The first team to all run through and end up ahead of where they started but in their original order wins.

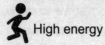 High energy

Ships and Lifeboats

Following orders upon the seven seas

Age: 6 and up

Players: 12 and up

What you need: Nothing

How to play: Play in a large rectangular space. The near end is Ships, the far end Lifeboats, the side to the players' left Port, the side to their right Starboard. The person in charge – the Captain – barks orders and all the players have to run to that point. The last person to do so is out. Play until just one sailor remains.

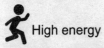 High energy

501 *Man overboard! Join him in the watery depths by playing Sharks and Minnows [238].*

Advanced Ships and Lifeboats

At Olympic level, this game is played with additional commands. 'Captain's Aboard' requires standing up straight and saluting. 'Heave ho' requires miming pulling up an anchor, while 'Man overboard' necessitates a bit of swimming.

 High energy

Pirate Ships and Lifeboats

One thing pirates hate is following orders. Those galleons are wall-to-wall rule-breakers. Any time a direction is shouted, players have to run to any of the other three sides. However, after a while, commands will get more complex – 'Starboard Ships!' means, for a pirate, heading swiftly to the corner of Port and Lifeboats.

 High energy

Rob the Nest

Steal from other teams, but make sure to strike a balancing act between which ones you rob

Age: 6 and up

Players: 12 and up

What you need: Six tennis balls, four hula hoops or buckets

How to play: Place the four hoops out forming a large square, 10 or so metres wide. Split into four even teams, with one standing behind each hoop, and place the balls in the centre of the square. The aim of the game is to get three or more balls into your hoop at once, but nobody is allowed to hold more than one ball at once, and until your first ball arrives, only one team member is allowed to leave the corner. Once you have one ball in your hoop, feel free to steal from other teams' hoops, but never holding more than one ball per person. The first team to manage to get three balls in their hoop at once (and loudly shout about it) wins.

 High energy

Buzz Off, Hairy Legs!

A group spelling game with a cheerfully silly pay-off

Age: 6 and up

Players: 15 and up

What you need: Nothing

How to play: The players form a circle. The person in charge says a word and points to one player, who says the first letter of it. The next player says the next letter, and so on. When the word is complete, the next player says 'Buzz', the one after that says 'Off', the one after that says 'Hairy', the one after that says 'Legs' and the one after that is out and sits down. If a player gets the letter wrong, they also sit down and a new word starts with the next player. Keep playing until only one player is standing.

 Low energy

> **501** *Nobody likes buzzing more than bees. Draw one of their insect pals in Beetle [378].*

Bucket Shuttle

Tactics, speed and splashing

Age: 6 and up

Players: Up to 20

What you need: Two buckets and one cup per team

How to play: Teams of five or so line up behind a bucket full of water, with another, empty, bucket a reasonable distance away – 10 or so metres. The person at the front of each line has a cup and, on the signal, fills it with water, runs to the empty bucket, tips the water in, runs back and passes their cup to the next player. The first team to fill the bucket wins. There are tactics to think about – do you go for speed and risk slopping loads out? Or do you walk steadily, risking being lapped, then sprint back when spillage isn't a concern?

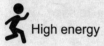 High energy

Connect-the-Kids

Use string and spoons to make a child kebab

Age: 6 and up

Players: Up to 20

What you need: String, spoons

How to play: Line up in teams of about five. The person at the front of each team is given a spoon tied to the end of a long piece of string. When a signal is given, the spoon has to be fed down through the first person's clothes in each team, up through the next person's clothes and so on, resulting in a five-person connected string.

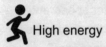 High energy

501 *If a confusing mess of limbs is what you're after, try Pretzel [303].*

Cup Firefighters

A firefighting chain that has to work together

Age: 6 and up

Players: Up to 40 (!)

What you need: A cup each, two buckets per team

How to play: Form teams of ten or so. Teams stand in side-by-side lines with everyone holding a cup, a full bucket at one end and an empty one at the other. By pouring water from one cup to the next as smoothly and efficiently as possible (handing the cup from person to person is not allowed), who can be the first to fill their empty bucket?

 High energy

501 *Use these cups to test your memory skills with Under the Cups Memory [288].*

Tiny Cup Firefighters

Use two different sizes of cup, alternating team members. Teams will have to figure out how to avoid letting this completely mess up the system – how fast does the person with the littlest cup have to work to avoid a bottleneck?

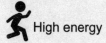 High energy

The Fearless Funambulist

All the skill of high-wire tightrope-walking without any of the pesky height

Age: 7 and up

Players: 2 and up, plus a referee

What you need: Tape or chalk, a blindfold, a timer

How to play: Draw a route on the ground with chalk. Form teams of two in which one blindfolded funambulist (a needlessly fancy word for tightrope-walker) is assisted by one extremely useful navigator. The referee keeps time, as well as shouting 'Foul!' every time the blindfolded funambulist goes off course. Each foul adds 2 seconds to the team's final time.

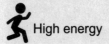 High energy

> **501** *Test balance skills even further with Fighting Chickens [144].*

Fizz Buzz

Like maths but very, very silly

Age: 7 and up

Players: 6 and up

What you need: Enough room to form a circle

How to play: Everyone stands in a circle and takes it in turns to count, one number at a time. But, instead of any multiple of three, you say fizz, and instead of any multiple of five, you say buzz. So person one says one, person two says two, person three says fizz, person four says four, person five says buzz, person six says fizz. Fifteen, as a multiple of both, is fizz-buzz. Start again from one if someone gets it wrong. After a few practice runs, because it takes some getting used to, start eliminating people and upping the speed.

 Low energy

501 *Fancy taking buzzing even further? Give the game Buzz Off, Hairy Legs [370] a go!*

Fizz Buzz Mmmmmm

Maths whizzes or general reckless geniuses can throw in mmmmmm for multiples of seven, and keep the numbers going up after players are eliminated. One, two, fizz, four, buzz, fizz, mmmmmm, eight, fizz, buzz, eleven, fizz, thirteen, mmmmmm, fizz-buzz. Twenty-one, for instance, would then be buzz-mmmmmm. You might even get as far as 105, which is a multiple of three, five and seven, so is fizz-buzz-mmmmmm. Ridiculous.

 Low energy

Stand Up Sit Down

A big group game that can be tailored to any maths level

Age: 7 and up

Players: 10 and up

What you need: Nothing

How to play: Pick a number – say, 25 – and tell everyone to sit down if the answer is less, and stand up if it is more. Everyone starts off crouching. Start off by just saying numbers themselves, but gradually make it trickier – go from '24' to 'two 13s' to 'hours in a day' to 'half a deck of cards'. Go as off-piste and convoluted as you like depending on who's playing. Anyone who does the wrong thing is out. Keep going, getting faster and more and more difficult, until only one person remains.

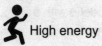 High energy

Sit in the Past

The same kind of game, but with historical events. Pick a date – the Millennium, perhaps, or the birth of one of the people at the party – and tell people to sit down if an event you name happened before it, and stand if it happened after it.

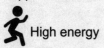 High energy

Beetle

Chance and art combine in an insectoid journey

Age: 7 and up

Players: Up to 20

What you need: Pencil, paper, dice

How to play: Sit in teams of four or five, with pencil and paper in the middle of each team, and one dice per team. When the game starts, each team starts throwing the dice, going round and round until someone throws a six, at which point the person who threw it draws a big oval – a beetle's thorax. You can add legs to the body by throwing ones (one leg each time), and an abdomen by throwing four. You can't add the head (five) until the abdomen is done, and you can't do eyes (two) or antennae (three) until you have a head. The winning team is the first to draw a complete beetle with a head, thorax and abdomen, two eyes, two antennae and six legs.

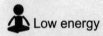 Low energy

501 *Combine those dice with truth-stretching in Liars' Dice [39].*

Alien

Why should members of the order Coleoptera have all the fun when there are extra-terrestrials desperate to get involved? Instead of a beetle, draw the surface of a planet when you roll a six, two legs (ones), a body (four), two arms (threes), a head (two) and three eyes (fives). Finish up with another six for the mouth to win.

 Low energy

Goth Dice

Why should extra-terrestrials and members of the order Coleoptera have all the fun when there are skulls everywhere desperate to get involved? Draw the outline of a skull when you get a six, eyes from fives, one nose cavity per four, a three for a bottom jaw, four teeth from rolling twos, and you can't finish without a one to add each eyeball and bring the skull to life.

 Low energy

Clothes Peg Assassin

An ongoing, running-in-the-background game of deviousness and timing

Age: 7 and up

Players: Any number

What you need: A clothes peg each, pens, paper, a bag

How to play: Everyone writes their name on a clothes peg and a piece of paper. The pieces of paper are then mixed up in the bag and given out. The piece of paper you get is the name of your victim, and at some point over the course of the day, you have to try and attach your peg to their clothing without them realising, and return their name to the bag, which is periodically checked. If you get caught doing it, your victim can take your peg and demand the paper, rendering you retired from the Assassins' Guild. Try to complete your mission and make it to the end of the day both unassassinated and unretired.

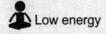 Low energy

Sticker Bandit

Everyone starts with a sticker on their back with a number on it. By the end of the day (or a prearranged time), whoever has collected the most of those stickers, folded them in half and pocketed them wins – however, if you are caught in the process of taking someone's sticker, you have to hand over all the ones you've amassed.

 Low energy

Hiero-Triffics

A game of quick drawing, quick thinking and quick guessing

Age: 8 and up

Players: 10 and up

What you need: Pens and paper, a timer, a large pad or easel, two bags

How to play: Split into two teams. Each team spends 5 minutes writing titles of films, songs and TV shows onto scraps of paper, which are then put in a bag and given to the other team. Players then take it in turns to take a piece of paper out and try to communicate it to their team in 30 seconds, entirely via the medium of drawing. No letters or numbers can be used, and no speaking is allowed.

 Low energy

Express Hiero-Triffics

Players have 1 minute to score as many points as they can, but only using one sheet of paper – careless but talented players might find themselves trying to somehow transform an excellent drawing representing *Jurassic Park* into one representing 'Shake It Off' by Taylor Swift.

 Low energy

Idiom Hiero-Triffics

Rather than using titles of films and the like, go for popular expressions and phrases. How do you go about drawing 'ignorance is bliss', for instance?

 Low energy

Elite Hiero-Triffics

Confident players who find the normal way of playing to be slightly too pedestrian for them can play Elite Hiero-Triffics – all the usual rules, but all drawing must be done with the non-dominant hand.

 Low energy

Back-and-Forth Hiero-Triffics

Drawing and writing combine to really confuse matters

Age: 8 and up

Players: 4 to 8

What you need: Pens, paper, a timer

How to play: Fold the paper into as many sections as you have players (you can also use multiple sheets of paper). The first player starts off by drawing an image representing a phrase or title on their section, for which they have 30 seconds. The second player looks at the drawing then folds it over and writes what they think it is in their section in 30 seconds. Then the third looks at what's been written and draws in theirs, and so on. Even with the best art and art-interpretation skills in the world, by a few steps in everything will have become nonsense.

 Low energy

All-Art Back-and-Forth Hiero-Triffics

As above, but without the writing – player one's picture reinterpreted by player two, reinterpreted by player three, and so on.

 Low energy

Acting the Goat

Performing skills are put to the test as figures of speech must be acted out

Age: 8 and up

Players: 4 and up

What you need: Pre-prepared cards with idioms and expressions on, a timer

How to play: Players take it in turns to act out as many of the expressions as they can in 1 minute. They don't have to be silent like in charades, but if speaking they do have to avoid using any of the words in the expression.

 Low energy

Describing the Goat

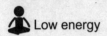

Players who'd rather not act can instead describe the expression, again avoiding using any of the words in it. You end up with catchy, laboured descriptions of figures of speech like 'Very similar, as similar as a pair of small green ball-shaped vegetables sharing a sort of capsule thing'.

 Low energy

Strings and Roundabouts

A good old-fashioned yarn

Age: 8 and up

Players: 4 and up

What you need: A ball or two of string or wool

How to play: Cut the string into various lengths – anything from 20 centimetres to a metre and a half – and distribute the bits over as wide a space as is available. Players have 5 minutes to find as much string as possible, but are not allowed to pick a new piece up until all the string they're holding is tied together. At the end, everyone's string is measured, and the person with the longest wins.

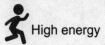 High energy

Team Mannequin

A silly, silly game of puppeteers and the puppets they control

Age: 8 and up

Players: 4 and up

What you need: Nothing

How to play: Players form teams of two. One is the puppeteer, one is the mannequin. The mannequin doesn't move at all, while the puppeteer can position them however they wish. The person in charge makes up a story, and every time they mention any sort of physical action or position, the puppeteer has to move their mannequin into that position. There isn't really a winner – it's just all very, very silly.

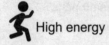 High energy

Giant's Soup

A certain degree of wetness is guaranteed in this game of communication skills and ping-pong balls

Age: 8 and up

Players: 4 and up

What you need: Two big buckets or pots, a ladle, a blindfold, ping-pong balls

How to play: Split into pairs. Position the buckets 3 metres or so apart. Fill the one furthest from the players with water and drop ping-pong balls to float in it. One pair at a time get 1 minute to transfer as many ping-pong balls from the far bucket to the close one as possible using the ladle, but the player holding the ladle is blindfolded and the one who isn't blindfolded can't touch anything.

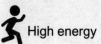 High energy

Back-to-Back Race

An extremely skilful way of racing that is about as tiring a way of travelling short distances as you'll ever find

Age: 8 and up

Players: 4 and up

What you need: Nothing

How to play: Form teams of two, and stand back to back, linking arms. Run the race between two points by taking it in turns to bend over, lifting your teammate on your back, and pivoting around to gain as much ground as possible.

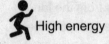 High energy

Wheelbarrow Race

Age: 8 and up

Players: 4 and up

What you need: Nothing

How to play: Form teams of two. One person puts their hands down on the ground in a push-up position, and the other lifts that player's legs up to their waist. A normal race then ensues, but the players at the front of the wheelbarrows are essentially crawling as fast as they can, half inverted.

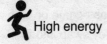 High energy

Bird, Beast, Fish

What Charles Darwin would play if he were a kid today

Age: 8 and up

Players: 6 and up

What you need: Nothing

How to play: One player stands in the middle while the others surround them. The person in the middle spins around chanting 'Bird, beast, fish . . .', then points at one person and demands a bird, beast or fish. They then start counting down from five, and if the person they pointed at can't come up with an answer, they are eliminated. If they do, they swap into the middle. The winner is the last player standing.

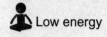 Low energy

The Unseeing Artist

Can your partner recreate a picture based only on your description?

Age: 8 and up

Players: 6 and up

What you need: Pens and paper, plus some prepared pictures – printouts from the internet, pages from books, pizza takeaway menus, anything

How to play: Split into teams of two, who sit back to back in a line. All the players on one side are given a picture, which they have 2 minutes to describe to their teammate (who has a pen and paper to try to copy it without seeing), without using any specific words. So, if it's a picture of a cat, not only can they not say cat, they can't mention that the shapes they're describing are ears or a tail or anything like that. They have to just work with shapes – 'Draw a circle that fills the left third of the paper, then add two triangles to the top of the circle' and so on.

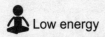 Low energy

Minimalist Rounders

Don't let not having a team stop you playing team sports

Age: 8 and up

Players: 6 and up

What you need: One bat, one ball and four bases – pretty much anything can work as a base

How to play: Arrange the bases in a diamond shape with equal sides of three or so metres. One person bats, one bowls, one stands behind the batter as backstop/fourth base and the other three are base people and fielders. If, after hitting the ball and running anti clockwise around the bases, the batter has to stop on a base (say, second), they then go and bat again and run straight to the next base (third) instead of starting again from the first. Score 1 for every completed rounder, and players stay in bat until they are caught or stumped out. Rotate positions as much as possible so nobody gets stuck, always facing the deadliest bowler.

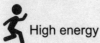 High energy

501 *Want to go even more lo-fi? Landfill Baseball [411] takes sports into a post-apocalyptic world.*

Actual Rounders

Ten people is enough for a proper game of rounders, although 20 or so is ideal. Form two teams. One bats, one fields. Players have to run if they hit the ball, and only one player can stick on each base at once. One point per completed rounder, and a team is in bat until everyone is out.

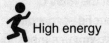 High energy

Slow-Motion Football

A lighter, floatier, heads-only version of soccer

Age: 8 and up

Players: 6 and up, ideally 10 or so

What you need: A balloon, something to mark goals with

How to play: Split into two teams. Most of the rules of football apply, except you can only use your head (hands must remain behind your back at all times), you use a balloon instead of a football and you can't run. Actually, now that it's written down, not a lot of the rules of football apply. Still, try to score goals solely by heading the balloon from slow-moving positions. There's a surprising amount of skill involved. Warning: don't play outside on a windy day, you'll lose your ball in a heartbeat.

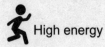 High energy

Connecting Cards

Aka 'human sculpture'

Age: 8 and up

Players: 8 and up

What you need: Cards, prepared beforehand, each with two body parts on

How to play: Form teams of four or so. Teams take one card at a time from the pile and have to grip the card between the two body parts listed – something that may require more than one person. Keep going until the whole team is involved and no more cards can be held – and watch out for mean-spirited cards saying things like 'mouth and bottom'. Score 1 point per successfully held card.

 Low energy

Domino Body Parts

Instead of prepared cards, use randomly selected dominoes, where each number (and blank) represents a different body part, i.e. ones are hands, twos are backs and so on.

 Low energy

Chessboxing

No chess, no boxing, but the same philosophy: combining physical and intellectual tasks

Age: 8 and up

Players: 8 and up

What you need: Paper, pens, pre-prepared puzzles – one per piece of paper, ranging from basic sums to more complex puzzles, depending on who's playing

How to play: Form teams of four or so, and line up. Place the puzzles, grouped by team, as far away as you can. At the signal, the first player in each team has to run to the end, choose one of the puzzles from their team's selection, finish it (ideally with someone there to check they've done it properly) and run back. The people further back in each team are at a disadvantage as they have less choice of challenge, so teams are encouraged to think tactically about what order to play in.

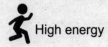 High energy

Deluxe Chessboxing

Instead of puzzles and sums, use items that need a bit of physical manipulation – put these six bits of LEGO together into a tower, make this piece of paper into an aeroplane, arrange these bricks in order from largest to smallest, move these marbles from one bowl to another using chopsticks, and so on.

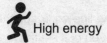 High energy

399

Balls in the Bucket

How good is your sense of direction when blindfolded? What about when blindfolded and being shouted at?

Age: 8 and up

Players: 10 and up

What you need: Each team needs a bucket, a blindfold, a serving spoon and a ping-pong ball, plus you need one more bucket and a chair.

How to play: Split into teams of four or five, each lined up behind an empty bucket, with another bucket on a chair 5 metres or so ahead, containing the balls. The player at the front of the line must put the blindfold on, take the spoon and spin around three times before making their way to the bucket of balls, relying both on their sense of direction and shouted help from their team. They need to then carry the ball back on the spoon – with their teammates directing them to pick it up if it falls – and deposit it in their bucket before passing the blindfold and spoon to the next player, who will return it. Alternatively, put as many fun-size chocolate bars in the far bucket as there are team members.

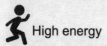 High energy

501 *To get more use out of that blindfold, try The Fearless Funambulist [374].*

Foot-Down Face-Off

Push! Push! Push!

Age: 8 and up

Players: 10 and up

What you need: Nothing

How to play: Players are split into two teams, and line up opposite one another about 60cm apart, reaching their hands out in front of them and touching hands with their opponent, palm to palm. Every pair is given a number. When that number is called, players push the hands of their opponent, trying to throw them off balance enough that they have to move their feet. If a player moves their feet, the other team scores 1 point. However, as soon as the next number is called, all other numbers have to stop pushing.

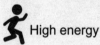 High energy

Foot-Down Face-off Frenzy

The person in charge can start adding extra elements – instead of just shouting one number out, they might shout a combination ('One, three, ten!'), or describe the numbers in a more confusing way ('Square root of 25!'), making being caught by surprise all the more likely.

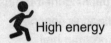 High energy

Noah's Ark

A great icebreaker game for the beginning of a party

Age: 8 and up

Players: 12 and up

What you need: Pre-prepared scraps of paper listing different animals – two of each

How to play: Everyone takes a piece of paper from the bag and, without talking but only using noises and actions to embody their animals, players must find their partners.

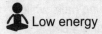 Low energy

> **501** *Enjoying making silly noises? Turn it into a big game with Fizz Buzz [375].*

End Zone

Like American Football without the pads, kicking or running

Age: 8 and up

Players: 12 and up

What you need: Three or more tennis balls

How to play: Split into two teams, with an adult referee. Designate end zones at opposite ends of the playing area. One team (toss a coin) starts off in the centre with all the balls – ideally, you want about half as many balls as team members. The aim is to score points by catching balls while standing in the end zone – running while holding a ball is strictly forbidden. The team moves forward by throwing the balls back and forth, moving between throws, while the other team tries to intercept the balls. When a point is scored, the ball is left on the floor in the end zone for the opposing team and the player who scored runs and slaps the referee's hand – no slap, no point.

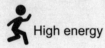 High energy

End Zone Frenzy

To really keep people on their toes, try playing where instead of having multiple identical tennis balls, every item in play is different. One tennis ball, one Frisbee, one basketball . . . How quickly can you all change modes? Can you throw a Frisbee and catch a basketball in one fluid movement?

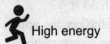 High energy

Bobbing for Apples

A needlessly difficult game beloved by Americans at Halloween

Age: 8 and up

Players: Any number

What you need: Large buckets, at least one apple per player

How to play: Fill the buckets with water and float the apples in them. For large groups, split into teams and have one bucket per team, treating it as a relay, but for smaller numbers, just do the one and take it in turns. Players have to retrieve the apples from the water using only their teeth, keeping their hands behind their backs at all times.

 High energy

String 'Em Up

A drier way to play. Core the apples, then string them up between two poles – enough for one per team member on each string, like a fruity washing line. Players will have to combine biting and pulling to be able to go back to their teams, apple in mouth.

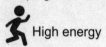 High energy

Mute Meeting

How many ideas can you come up with as a group if you aren't allowed to talk?

Age: 9 and up

Players: 12 and up

What you need: Pens and paper

How to play: Split into groups of four or five. The whole group will be given a category, and each group has to come up with ten things in that category without speaking to one another, but doing as much in the way of charades and mime as is necessary, with only one person writing. When a team has ten answers, they stand up.

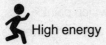 High energy

Guggenheim

Hours and hours of intense competition as everyone tries to out-unique one another

Age: 10 and up

Players: 3 and up

What you need: Paper and pens

How to play: Start by deciding on ten categories, which every player writes down the side of their answer sheet, drawing vertical lines to give themselves answer columns (one column per round, and as many rounds as there are players). Each round begins with a player randomly selecting a letter (opening a book with eyes closed, twirling a finger and jabbing it down is one way of doing this), at which point everyone has 2 minutes to come up with an answer in every category starting with that letter. Go through everyone's answers after each round. Double-initialled answers (e.g. San Sebastian, Marilyn Monroe) score 2 points. However, only unique answers score any points at all – if two of you come up with the same answer, it's a 0. The player with the most points after everyone has initiated a round wins.

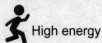 High energy

Opening Gala

Collectively choose a way of describing where you are, what the occasion is or why you're all together – anything from BIRTHDAY to NELL'S HOUSE. Write it down across your paper with a column for each letter. Then take it in turns to name a category (or randomly select one from a big list), giving everyone 2 minutes (or longer if necessary) to come up with an answer for each.

 Low energy

Keep It Brief

How much can you describe using words of one syllable? Can you even describe a syllable in one-syllable words? No!

Age: 10 and up

Players: 4 and up

What you need: Pencil and paper, bags

How to play: Split into two teams. Each team spends 5 minutes writing films, songs and famous people on pieces of paper, then give them to the other team. Players have to describe the clues given to them only using one-syllable words and none of the words from the titles, a difficult task leading to could-mean-anything descriptions like 'A film with things with big teeth in'.

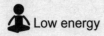 Low energy

Landfill Baseball

Repurpose rubbish into sporting equipment, then recycle it

Age: 10 and up

Players: 6 and up

What you need: Drinks cans or plastic bottles, a stick or bat, a hula hoop or circle drawn on the ground

How to play: One player stands behind the hoop with the stick, while the other players stand behind a line about 4 metres away, each with a can. One at a time, they try to throw their can into the hoop. The stick-holder protects the hoop with the stick. However, if the can is hit and lands on the ground, the person who threw it can throw it again from where it landed. Keep playing until everyone's can is in the hoop, the stick-holder scoring 1 point for every throw, then rotate stick-holders. When everyone has been, if the top score is shared by multiple players, they each have another innings until there is a clear winner.

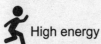 High energy

501 *For another stripped-back version of a massive sport, try Pencil Hockey [98].*

Who Am I?

The names-on-forehead classic

Age: 10 and up

Players: 8 and up

What you need: Post-it notes, pre-written

How to play: Everyone is given a Post-it with a famous person's name on it – these can be drawn at random, or specifically written with individual players in mind. Without looking at them, they stick the note to their forehead. Everyone's goal is to work out who they are by asking other people questions, either one at a time as a turn-based thing, or more informally as a mingling icebreaker activity.

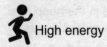 High energy

Wink Murder

Holmes. Marple. Poirot. Fletcher. Insert surname here.

Age: 10 and up

Players: 8 and up

What you need: Nothing, although some way of selecting a murderer can come in handy

How to play: One player is selected as the murderer – one quick way of doing this is getting the same amount of cards as there are players, naming one card (say, the ace of spades) as the murderer card, and handing them out, ensuring nobody sees one another's. The murderer then tries to make eye contact with people and wink at them. Someone who is winked at must wait a few seconds and 'die', as dramatically as they want (think shrieking, falling, pretending to vomit, etc). If someone feels they have witnessed a murder and can identify the killer, they shout 'I accuse!' If nobody else has seen it, play carries on (although that person might want to avoid making eye contact with the killer). If someone else feels they've seen the killer too, they say 'I second!', then after a countdown from three they both point to the killer. If they point to the same person, and that person is indeed the killer, they have caught the murderer and won. If they point to different people, they both die – again, as loudly and dramatically as they see fit. As soon as there are only two people left alive, the murderer has won. What a *rotter*!

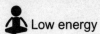 Low energy

Wink Detective

At the same time as secretly selecting a murderer, a detective is also selected. The detective is the only person who can accuse the murderer, but they can make a maximum of three false accusations before being thrown off the force.

 Low energy

Ball Relay

A simple combination of running and throwing to get the blood pumping or make everyone sleepy

Age: 10 and up

Players: 8 and up

What you need: One ball per team

How to play: Form teams of four or so. Teams stand behind a line, and another line is drawn 10 metres ahead of them. The first player holds the ball and, on the signal, runs to the line then throws the ball back to the second player, who runs to join them and throws it back to the third, and so on. Each time the whole team changes ends counts as 1 point. The team with the most points after 2 minutes wins.

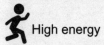 High energy

Dribble Relay

The 'run over there, send something back to someone who runs over there and sends it back' model is pretty adaptable. Dribbling a football then hoofing it back to teammates, running with a Frisbee then elegantly floating it back to teammates, swimming the length of a pool holding a tennis ball and throwing it back . . . Endless variations, depending on where you are and what you've got.

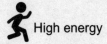 High energy

Tug of War

Brute force, standing your ground and heave-ho-ing as a team

Age: 10 and up

Players: 8 and up

What you need: A rope about 6 metres long, a ribbon

How to play: Form two teams. Make a mark on the floor (or use one that's already there) as the centre line, and position a team on either side of it, holding the rope, with the ribbon tied around it above the centre line. On the signal, both teams have to try to pull the whole opposing team over the centre line. Be careful – risks with this game involve rope burn and falling.

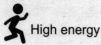 High energy

Venom

There's poison running through your veins

Age: 10 and up

Players: 12 and up

What you need: Paper and pens, a bag

How to play: Put as many scraps of paper in the bag as there are players, but mark a quarter of them with a big X. Everyone takes one out and looks at it without letting anyone else see. Anyone who gets an X is infected with Venom and must try to pass it on. Everyone mills around, shaking hands with one another, but those infected with Venom tap people on the wrist, subtly, twice while shaking. If you are tapped, at some point within the next 10 seconds you need to do a big theatrical 'death'. If two infected people tap one another, neither die. If you are uninfected and think you can identify someone who is, loudly shout and accuse them – if you're right, they die, but if you're wrong, you do. The game ends when only the original infectees are alive.

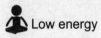 Low energy

Chalk Rugby

A very physical game for bigger kids

Age: 12 and up

Players: 10 and up

What you need: Coloured chalk, paper, tape

How to play: Play indoors in as wide open a space as possible. Split into two teams. Tape a piece of A4 paper to the floor at either end of the 'field'. Teams score points by marking Xs on the paper, which they do by barging their way through one another, passing the chalk back and forth and wrenching the chalk off the other team when possible.

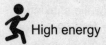 High energy

> 501 *That chalk can be put to much more peaceful use with Human Boules [342].*

Index

ball games 120–35
 Butts Up 135
 Donkey 127
 Doubles Downball 124
 Downball 123
 Eliminate 7, 121
 Four Square 126
 Headers and Volleys 131
 High, High, Up in the Sky 129
 Horse 127
 Jumbo Catch 133
 Jumbo Turbo Catch 133
 Long-Distance Battleship 130
 More Square 126
 Paddling Pool Battleship 130
 Piggy in the Middle 120
 Pork and Mash 120
 Post-Apocalypse Golf 125
 Runs 132
 Super Jumbo Turbo Catch 134
 Wally 128, 224
 World Cup 122
 World Cup of Everything 122
beach games 244–53
Beach Channel Tunnel 225, 248
Bucket Spoof 251
Buried Legs Olympics 250
Castle Cannon 247
Crab Football 253
International Bucket Spoof 252
Leaky Lifesaver 245
Pebble Petanque 246
Pooh Sticks 244
Slow But Steady 248
Throwing the Square 225, 249

card games 50–86
 Bad Neighbours 86
 Beggar My Neighbour 6, 59
 Big-hand Rummy 81

California Spit 83
Card Dominoes 73
Change 62
Chase the Ace 57
Cheat 78
Cheerful Cheat 79
Devilishly Difficult Diplomat 77
Diplomat 76
Famous Families 75
Global Skirmish 51
Go Fish 58
Happy Families 74
Higher or Lower 63
Irish Snap 56
Knacker Your Neighbour 85
Light Rummy 80
Literature 84
Little Trumps 71
Memory 52
Memory Deluxe 52
My Ship Sails 65
Mystery Maid 61
Old Maid 61
One Fish 58
Put Your Finger on Your
 Nose 66
Ratkiller 60
Rolling Stone 64
Schnipp Schnapp Schnorem 54
Silent Sevens 56
Skirmish 50
Slapjack 55
Snap 55
Snip Snap Snorem 53
Spit 6, 82
Spoon Quest 67
Thirty-One 72
24 69
24 Hours 70
Uno 68

dice/coin games 33–49
   Chickenfoot 46
   Dice 404 48
   Dice Himalaya 35
   Dice Mountain 34
   Dice 101 48
   Fifty-Headed Monster 33
   Five Coins and a Cup 42
   54321 36
   Fünfzehn 38
   Liars' Dice 39
   Macau 38
   Mia 47
   Pair of Liars, A 40
   Pair of Pigs, A 44
   Pig 44
   Sevens, Elevens and Doubles 41
   Shift Right 45
   Ship, Captain and Crew 37
   Spin the Sovereign 43
   Three Heads and Three Tails 33
   Yacht 49

hand games 214–21
   Chopsticks 220
   Cow, Lake, Bomb 215
   Hoi Sai 219
   Morra 221
   Odds and Evens 216
   Rock, Paper, Nitwit 215
   Rock, Paper, Scissors 214
   Slaps 218
   Thumb War 217
holiday games 3, 222–53 see also
   individual game name
   beach games 244–53 see also
     beach games
   swimming pool games 226–43
     see also swimming pool games
   household items, games involving
     8–32
   Ball Blow-off 28
   Balloon Bomb 8
   Beasts in the Tundra 10
   Big Game Thimble Hunting 9
   Blindfolded Obstacle Course 16
   Blow Football 17
   Blow Skiing 17
   Can Clatter 25

Catch My Drift 26
DIY Bowling 6, 14
Five Pence Hockey 27
Floor is Lava, The 11
Floor is Lava and the Lava has
   Monsters, The 12
Great Sock Hunt, The 22
Hallway Curling 32
Hot and Cold 13
Hunt the Thimble 9
Laundry-Basket Horse 21
Metre Made 31
Non-stop Pick-up Pasta 23
Obstacle Course 16
Paper Rugby 29
Pick-up Pasta 23
Professional DIY Bowling 15
Racin' Riches, Rollin' Ramps 24
Scavenger Hunt 18
Show-Off Scavengers 20
Snow Blower 26
Sock Wrestling 30
Super Secret Sock Search 22
Teeny-Tiny Treasure Trove 19
Thoughtful Scavenger, The 18

indoor games 2–3, 5–115
   card games 50–87 see also card
     games
   dice/coin games 33–49 see also
     dice/coin games
   household items, games involving
     8–32 see also household items,
     games involving
   pencil-and-paper games 87–115
     see also pencil-and-paper
     games
   see also individual game name

looking out the window games
   194–213
   Bus Stop 197
   Colonel, The Clown and the King,
     The 149, 207
   Competitive Car Collecting 212
   Competitive Collecting Carousel
     212
   Counting Colours 204
   Cryptic I Spy 195

Cursed Colours 204
I Find, In My Clever Mind 196
I Spy With My Particularly Little
    Eye 195
I Spy, With My Little Eye 194
Letters in the Wild 199
Mine! 201
Motorway Multiplex 210
Motorway Nemesis 205
Nouns 208
Now! 201
Number Plate Baseball 211
Number Plate Encapsulate 213
Number Plate Nicknames 149, 210
Pub Cricket 209
Pub Test Match 209
Service Station Scavenger Hunt
    206
Three For a Freestyle Pig 201
Three For a Pig 149, 202
Three For an Octopus 203
Twinspotting 198
Verbing 200
Wild World of Words 199
World is a Rainbow, The 198

outdoor games 3, 117–45
    ball games 120–35 see also ball
        games
    other equipment 136–45 see also
        individual game name

party and big group games 254–418
    big group/playground games
        258–80 see also playground/
        big group games
    party games/adult in charge
        281–418 see also party games/
        adult in charge
Acting the Goat 386
Actual Rounders 395
Advanced Ships and Lifeboats
    367
Alien 379
All-Art Back-and-Forth Hiero-
    Triffics 385
Animal Acrostic 364
Are You Feline Competitive?
    297

Back-and-Forth Hiero-Triffics 384
Back-to-Back Race 390
Ball Relay 415
Balloon Burst 301
Balloon Kneelay 289
Balloon Relay 289
Balls in the Bucket 400
Beetle 378
Bing Bang Whoops 334
Bird, Beast, Fish 392
Blind Man's Buff 343
Bobbing for Apples 406
Box of Delights 314
Breakaway 332
Bucket Shuttle 371
Buff Mush 343
Bugged Lines 298
Buzz Off, Hairy Legs! 370
Card Toss 287
Catch the Dragon's Tail 257, 357
Cats and Mice 296
Chalk Rugby 418
Charades 323
Chessboxing 257, 398
Chopscotch 309
Chopstick Run 299
Chopsticks and Smarties 299
Clothes Peg Assassin 380
Commando Race 341
Connect-the-Kids 372
Connecting Cards 397
Cross-Country Leapfrog 339
Cup Firefighters 373
Dangling Deliciousness 307
Dangling Doughnuts 256, 307
Deluxe Chessboxing 399
Describing the Goat 386
Dice, Dice, Very Nice 285
Domino Body Parts 397
Dribble Relay 415
Duck Duck Goose 119, 345
Egg and Spoon Race 321
Egg on Your Face 321
Elite Hiero-Triffics 383
End Zone 404
End Zone Frenzy 405
European Rules Silent Ball 359
Express Charades 324
Express Hiero-Triffics 382

party games – *cont.*
Face Feel 344
Father Christmas and His Nice
Beard 286
Fearless Funambulist, The 374
Fish and Chips 256, 356
Fizz Buzz 375
Fizz Buzz Mmmmmm 376
Flour Power 316
Foot-Down Face-Off 401
Foot-Down Face-off Frenzy 402
Frozen Friends 349
Giant's Soup 389
Goth Dice 379
Green's on Fire 330
Guggenheim 224, 408
Hide and Seek 283
Hide and Seek Home 283
Hiero-Triffics 382
Hoop Relay 257, 340
Human Boules 342
Human Dartboard 327
Human Dartboard Doubles 328
Human Mirror 320
I, Fly 313
Ibble Dibble 331
Idiom Hiero-Triffics 383
Impression Charades 324
Keep It Brief 410
Kicking Rounders 358
Kim's Game 256, 318
Landfill Baseball 411
Limb Chaos 303
Long-Distance Soaking 284
Make Me a Masterpiece 360
Make Me a Mummy 335
Make Me an Exhibition 361
Many-Mouthed Marbles 317
Minimalist Rounders 394
Mint Toothpicks 365
Mouths and Marbles 257, 317
Mummy Race 335
Musical Bumps 348
Musical Chairs 292
Musical Dice Unlucky Explosion
351
Musical Potato 350
Musical Statues 257, 348
Musically Marooned 292

Mute Meeting 407
Noah's Ark 403
Opening Gala 409
Paired Piñata 310
Pass the Cards 355
Pass the Panama 282
Pass the Parcel 281
Pass the Sample 326
Pass the Sausage 354
Peg Pick-up 300
Peg Relay 300
Pin the Donkey on the Donkey
312
Pin the Tail on the Donkey 311
Pirate Ships and Lifeboats 368
Polos and Straws 365
Pretzel 257, 303
Real-World Spot the Difference 319
Rebellious Rule-Breakers 291
Rob the Nest 369
Sardines 290
Seat Scramble 346
Sharks and Desert Islands 329
Sharks and Minnows 238
Ships and Lifeboats 367
Shoe Shuttle 257, 352
Silent Ball 118, 359
Simon Says 291
Sit in the Past 377
Slow-Motion Football 396
Snowflake Race 338
Soak the Adult 284
Socks of Delight 314
Spider's Web 313
Stacked Sweetie Selection 306
Stand Up Sit Down 377
Sticker Bandit 381
Stony Silence 325
String 'Em Up 406
Strings and Roundabouts 387
Sweet, Sweet Memories 256, 315
Sweetie in a Haystack 305
Team Mannequin 388
Team Slalom 257, 366
Telephone 298
Tennis Neck 333
Territorial Balloons 353
Three-Legged Race 322
Thumbs Up 295

Tiny Cup Firefighters 373
Toe Tap 308
Toilet Paper Toes 355
Traffic Lights 294
Traffic Lights in Atlantis 294
Tug of War 416
Under the Cups Memory 288
Under the Sea 362
Unseeing Artist, The 393
Venom 417
Water Balloon Piñata 310
What a Cairo-on 336
What's Missing? 318
What's the Time, Mr Wolf? 293
Wheelbarrow Race 391
Who Am I? 412
Whoozit 363
Wink Detective 414
Wink Murder 413
You Limb Sum, You Lose Some 304
You You Me 345
Zip Bong 302
Zip Bong X-Ray 302
Zombie Tag 337

pencil-and-paper games 87–115
Aquamarine Gun 115
Baddleship 90
Battleship 89
Bunch of Fives, A 106
Consequences 96
Cow-Words and Ver-Bulls 104
Cows and Bulls 104
Different Dots 99
Dots 99
Exquisite Corpse 92
Extended Tin Ha Tai Ping 95
Five by Five 100
Fives Fight 105
Galactic Spacebucks 113
Hang Out, Man 91
Hangman 91
Hockey Smile 98
Kropki 111
Nine Holes 88
Nine Men's Morris 102
Notakto 110
Organisation vs Anarchy 101
Pencil Hockey 98

Rare Danger 114
Salvo 90
Sliding Holes 88
SOS 97
Sprouts 112
Ten Men's Morris 103
Three Fifteen 107
Tic-Tac-Toe 87
Tic-Tac-Toenail 87
Tin Ha Tai Ping 94
Treble Cross 109
Tree of Delights 93
Ultimate Tic-Tac-Toe 108

playground/big group games 3, 258–80
Amoeba Tag 260
Ankle Tag 262
Bally Hey 261
Break the Gates 280
British Bulldog 7, 270
Bullrushes 271
Captain of the Compass 258
Capture the Flag 275
Chilly Dogs 272
Cops and Robbers 274
Crack the Whip 269
Duck Hunt 267
French Cricket 279
Half-Tag 261
Hopping Jinny 270
Hospital Tag 260
Hug in the Mud 263
Hunter and Guard 276
I Am Not a Number 277
Kick the Can 274
Mega Duck Hunt 268
Non-Stop Cricket 265
Octopus Tag 260
Pair Tag 261
Qiu 264
Red Rover 280
Reject This False World 278
Shadow Tag 259
Smugglers 266
Stuck in the Mud 7, 263
Tag 259
Team Bullrush 271
Two-Headed Bulldog 273

423

swimming pool games 226–43
  Airborne Alphabet 229
  Airborne Catch 225, 236
  Airborne Interrogation 229
  Almost Volleyball 240
  Beach Ball Bomb 228
  Chicken in the Middle 243
  Chickenfight 243
  Colour Tag 231
  Cursed Treasure 235
  Deep Voices 230
  Fruits de Mer 226
  Keep My Luggage Dry 237
  Marco Polo 225, 234
  Not Quite Polo 241
  Octopus Alert 232
  Sharks and Minnows 238
  Silent Ships 234
  Speedy Seafood 227
  Splash! 242
  Submarine Karaoke 230
  Sunken Treasure 235
  The Sinker 239
  Watery Whack-a-Mole 225, 233

travel games 3, 147–221
  hand games 214–21 *see also*
    hand games
  looking out the window games
    194–213 *see also* looking out
    the window games
  word games 150–93 *see also*
    word games

word games 150–93
  Alice, Belgian Cellist 191
  Alphabet Game, The 168
  Animal Psychiatrist 161
  Ask the Brain 163
  Bag Contains Doodahs, A 155
  Bureaucrat's Cat, Described
    Elegantly: Fairly Good, Huh, A
    166
  Botticelli 192
  Carnelli 189
  Celebrity Hangout 188
  Crambo 180
  El Fantasmo 182
  Eternal Alphabet 169

Everyone From Everywhere
  Loves Everything 190
Face-to-Face Fact-to-Fact 150
Fortunately/Unfortunately 160
Functions 176
Ghost 182
Hammersmith or Bust 159
Homophones 183
Hot Talent 185
I Packed My Bag 155, 224
In Common 174
Is It More Like . . . ? 175
Media Megastore 187
Meet in the Middle 162
Minister's Cat, The 165
Ministry of Everything 166
No More Dudes 184
Once Upon a Time 154
One-Minute Million 149, 178
One-Sentence Saga 153
One-Word Odyssey 153
Punlimited Entertainment 187
Questions 171
Rhyming Chain 167
Rhyming Nicknames 167
Russian Ambassador's Ball, The
  157
Say What You See 154
Sixty-Second Subject 179
Sixty Winks 159
Sorry I'm Late 164
Special List for a Special Day, A
  181
Stinkety Pinkety 186
Tongue-Tied Twenty 170
Top-Secret Password 158
Top-Secret Rule 158
21 156
21 And Over 156
Twenty Questions 170
Twenty-Second Treasure Trove
  149, 173
Two Truths and a Lie 177
Two Truths and a Tournament 177
Vermicelli 193
Word Dissociation 152
Wordhammer 151
Would You Rather . . . ? 172
Yes No Black White 157

Useful Tips

- All of these games are just ideas and starting points. Smash a few together, make up your own rules, give everything silly names, customise everything to your own family and surroundings, and generally make it all your own.

- Pretty much any game can be improved with the inclusion of food, loud noises and forfeits.

- A lot of these games involve using pennies for lives – swap those for something edible and you add an extra element of (depending on what you've chosen) nutrition or willpower.

- Bean bags are handy things to have, and they're pretty easy to make with a bit of fabric and some dried beans. Plus any game is that bit more special when you've made the things you're playing with. To make them a bit more robust, make an inner bag from muslin as well as a nicer-looking outer layer. Sew up the brunt of them before putting the beans in or you'll get beans everywhere and drive yourself nuts.

- You can get a bit more out of any game involving pencil and paper by spending a bit of time together decorating your sheets beforehand. No game ever suffered from being too pretty.

- Half the point of this is to use phones less, but they can help out, too: Siri or Google will throw a dice or flip a coin if you ask them to.

Acknowledgements

Enormous thanks to everyone who helped with this book, whether by suggesting games or listening to me talking endlessly about how 501 was a really high number. My amazing parents, Colin and Hilary Rampton, were incredibly helpful throughout, and suggested most of the good ones – I absolutely couldn't have written this book without them. Massive cheers also to my sisters Ellie and Vic, and by extension Charlie, Toby, Isla and Ted, for loads of brilliant ideas.

I am an organisational black hole, so a huge thank you to all of the actual, proper book people involved in this for their endless patience, whether by putting up with my very basic questions, politely suggesting I change some of the horror movie and death metal references or listening to my rambling excuses for missing deadlines. They include Laura Higginson, Sam Crisp and Lucie Humphrey at Pop Press, Zoë King and Julia Churchill at A.M. Heath and Julia Koppitz and Jenni Davis at whitefox. Apologies to anybody missing – please see 'organisational black hole' statement above.

Endless thanks to Freyja for putting up with me going half-mad writing this (and hijacking her annual leave to do so), and unlimited love forever to Phoenix, my magical little wonderful clever girl.